Wings of Light

The Art Of Angelic Healing

Wings of Light
The Art Of Angelic Healing

The Angels Xedah have transmitted these teachings
with the collaboration of
Marie Lise Labonté
channeler
and Ninon Prévost
author

Wings of Light
The Art of Angelic Healing
Copyright 1998 with Marie Lise Labonté
and Ninon Prévost
Cover design by:
ISBN#: 1-891099-04-3

Blue Pearl Press

4060 Morena Blvd., Suite 109G
San Diego, CA 92117

To order additional copies of this book call:

1-888-BOOKS-08

Printed in the United States Of America

*T*hose who read this book will be blessed, because this book contains sacred teachings transmitted by the Golden Word of the Angels.

The Angels: This term refers to a group of angels whose spokesperson is an entity by the name of Xedah. Marie Lise Labonté serves him as his human channel, or medium. The transmission of these messages takes place when the medium—often called "the form" by the angels—has obtained a profound trance state. The medium is called "animated" because these entities inhabit and animate their entire body, thus assuring a more complete communication. This group of angels are associated with Raphael, the Archangel of Healing.

We have chosen to transcribe as faithfully as possible the language of the angels. The teachings of the angels are presented in italics, and the text in roman typeface has been written by Ninon Prévost.

In this book, we do not reveal the specific steps involved in giving treatments, because they make up only a part of the specific teachings and initiations given by the master teachers of spiritual angelic healing.

Dedication

This book is dedicated to all the beings who help heal the soul and bring peace to this world.

Preface

In 1986, while I was giving a conference on the theme of healing to doctors and nurses, I was struck by Angelic Grace. I felt an energy enter my crown chakra with such a force that I almost lost consciousness. What scared me was that this energy was trying to communicate something to the doctors which was altogether different from what my brain was trying to communicate. Although it was painful and difficult, I tried to control this spiritual energy and to resume the usual course of my conference. I succeeded, but I was ignoring at that moment the fact that my life was starting to head in a completely different direction. Immediately afterwards, I felt inhabited by an energy which was coming from higher planes. For more than two years I resisted, struggled, and fought with myself, refusing this phenomenon that I was experiencing. I sought to understand what had happened to me during this conference and what I was experiencing every day since. I finally discovered that I had become the channel of an angelic energy of healing which was called The Angels Xedah, Xedah being the spokesperson for these angels.

These angels of healing were asking me, as a channel, to communicate in public meetings their teachings about a form of unique healing that acts on the subtle bodies and on the physical body, a form of healing which had already been practiced in ancient Egypt. During these transmissions, they spoke to us about an important energetic fluid upon which they could act, and they said it was necessary for humans to learn to regulate this fluid at the level of the subtle bodies. I didn't dare believe what the angels were communicating to me because, as a professional therapist, I was very skeptical and was afraid of losing my professional reputation.

I was, at this time, a psychotherapist and author of several books about the power of self-healing. I owned an important center in Montreal where I treated people who had attained psychosomatic illnesses. I was also recognized publicly (from interviews in the newspapers and appearances on television) for the work that I did in my community. So, it was very difficult for me to admit first of all that I had become a channel, and secondly, that I was channeling angels who wanted to offer their help and teach their healing through me, as their channeler. I was very afraid to ruin my reputation as a seasoned psychotherapist. The size of this challenge which I had to face appeared far too big for me; I refused for more than a year to channel what they wanted to communicate to me about healing, and I asked them for proof of their claims.

Finally, on the day before I was going to leave the country for a week of rest, I was with my editor looking at the books displayed in the show room of their publishing house, taking the opportunity to put my work in a prominent place. My author's ego was attracted by a book, translated from the American version, which had been placed in full view, hiding my books. I was hastening to take the book and put it elsewhere, when suddenly I noticed the title *Spiritual Healing* by Allan Young. Struck by some powerful force as soon as I started to put it back on the shelf, I decided to buy it and to take it with me on vacation.

During my vacation in the sun, my head well-rested, I took the book, and, "coincidentally" my attention fell on the chapter entitled, "Angelic Healing." To my great astonishment, the author gave a description of a type of healing practiced by angelic entities. This description corresponded almost totally to what I had received from the angels when I was channeling. The author said:

There are guardian angels who protect and guide us and healing angels who help transmit healing energy to those who ask for it. These healing angels fulfill their mission in large part by using a power (an energetic, regenerative and reparative fluid) to insure the functioning of the chakras, and they sometimes change certain substances in the physical, etheric and metaphysical bodies. They can direct toward the physical, etheric, and astral bodies a powerful ray of regenerative, vital, and purifying energy which comes from their aura and other reserves. This creates auspicious conditions for purification, or elimination, and healing.

(Young, Allan, *La guérison Spirituelle*, Ed. Québec Amérique, traduction 1990).

I had asked for proof, and I received a divine response. The Angels Xedah were right, and I could not recognize the truth of the information they were trying to communicate to me. Right then, I accepted their request to help them transmit this ritual of intervention.

It was during an intensive two-day workshop entitled "Love and Healing" that the angels transmitted to us this form of healing. These seminars comprised periods of prayer and meditation permitting the participants to integrate the treatments and to heighten their vibrational frequency to channel the angelic energy. Since this time, certain healers from Canada and Europe have been initiated by the Angels Xedah. They now transmit this form of healing throughout the entire world.

Spiritual angelic healing is not a method, but actually, a ritual of intervention where the healer becomes a pure tool that can channel the energy of angelic love and transmit this light. . . this love which heals.

This book contains both the angels' teachings, with explanations of spiritual angelic healing more commonly known as "Energetic Therapy," as well as the teachings of Ninon Prévost, a great friend of the Angels Xedah and a Master Teacher, initiated by them. Ninon gives us her vision, her experience, and the synthesis of her knowledge acquired from this type of healing. As a healer she has, through her private practice, touched hundreds of people with her light. The book ends with several case histories of people who have received the grace of spiritual angelic healing in the private practice of Ninon.

It is with great pleasure that I present this work to you, an anthology of the first level of intervention in spiritual angelic healing. I am very grateful to have been chosen as the channel of this energy of love. Enjoy this book with your heart and your consciousness.

—*Marie Lise Labonté*

Acknowledgments

I would like to thank Jean Bianchi for helping me to put my experiences into words and Gail Fairbank-Roch for supporting me in the translation of this text.

I would also like to thank my daughter Karine for her strength, encouragement, and love and for being my confidante during the making of this book.

—*Ninon Prévost*

I would like to thank all the healers trained by the Angels Xedah in Spiritual Angelic Healing for their precious work on the planet.

I would also like to thank the Angels Xedah, the Healing Angels for their guidance in my life and in the life of many human beings. May your Healing Grace be shared among us.

—*Marie Lise Labonté*

Table of Contents

Introduction

> "*True healing must happen through the soul because it is the soul which has chosen to be incarnated on the earth in order to confront the wounds accumulated during a number of past lives and to free himself from them once and for all.*"
>
> —*Ninon Prévost*

Ever since I can remember, I have been searching for love, because I have always recognized its great power. Love is like food. . . without love the heart withers and dies. So, for a long, long time this ceaseless pursuit kept my focus outward, looking for love relationships which, I thought, were going to bring me fulfillment. I firmly believed in the complete merging of two beings, and I aspired to find, in a romantic relationship, an experience of the absolute and great illumination.

I actually did experience very intense moments of true unity and tenderness, but when I was alone again, I would gradually feel even more empty than before. And my attachment to the other person, instead of fulfilling me, became the source of my suffering and pain.

After a particularly difficult break up, I took refuge in India with a spiritual master. Her radiant presence comforted me and helped me face my sadness by going deeply inside it and staying in touch with my wounded heart. I realized for the first time how empty I felt and how dependent I am on others to assure my happiness. At the same time as I felt this wound in my heart, I realized that every human being carries this same deep wound inside. I could see how delicate the human condition is. Yet, most incredibly, this realization, instead of making my heart close down, opened up a door inside of me. My soul, like a bird set free from its cage, suddenly revealed itself and filled the empty space inside me. Wave upon wave of bliss washed over me and for a moment I felt myself at one with the universe.

After this experience, my relationship with life and with others completely transformed. I had learned how to draw from the true source of love, compassion, and happiness. This source, to my great astonishment, was hidden inside of me and it was up to me now to remain in touch with this source forever! I was solely responsible for my own life and my own healing!

Seven years earlier, my spiritual master gave me the name Karuna, and a Tibetan lama had called me Richen Lamo. The former means compassion in Sanskrit, and the latter means The Goddess of Compassion. These names didn't mean much to me then, but after my stay in India, they took on a new meaning. I returned home with an ardent desire to help alleviate suffering. I didn't know how my type of service was going to unfold, but I was now listening to my inner being and soul, which was guiding me progressively toward the way of spiritual healing.

In the following few years, I studied and experimented with many different methods of healing, such as, polarity, hypnotherapy, naturopathy, healing methods of the Philippines, Chinese herbal medicine, healing with stones and crystals, Reiki, and, finally angelic intervention. These different techniques made me understand that the true healing must begin with the soul, because it is truly the soul which has chosen to be incarnated on this earth in order to confront the scars which have accumulated over a number of lifetimes. By confronting these scars, one becomes free of them forever.

At the very beginning of this work, I knew that divine guides of light were with me, surrounding me, but I didn't always feel their presence, nor was I aware of their actions. In the very core of my heart, I wanted to do my best, and I offered myself as a channel for the healing energy. But, in order to succeed, I was aware that I had to free myself from certain deep attachments which were still hindering me. It was then that the beings of healing began to manifest.

One morning, after my daily meditation, I was lying on the bed for a few minutes. I suddenly felt the presence of divine beings of love directly above me, and divine hands of light were penetrating my chest and beginning to tear out certain deep-seated emotions by the roots. The more the hands worked, the more I felt freed from the burden of emotions that had been strangling me; I had never known, until this moment, how I could ever clear them away.

When this episode was over, the oppressive weight had disappeared, creating in my heart a space in which to welcome an even larger love. I felt a cool, luminous liquid flowing from my head and spreading a balm throughout my chest and heart. Then, to my great surprise, I saw there was a garden of flowers—all the color of fuchsia—in my heart, and it was filling my entire chest. This experience was so tangible that I could almost touch the flowers and smell their beautiful fragrance.

When contemplating what had happened, I understood that these beings of light had heard my prayer, that their work on me had freed me from a part of my attachments, and that they had given me a magnificent proof of their existence. I wished once again to be able to understand and know their secrets and their ways of healing, but I knew intuitively that this knowledge was not in a human being's capacity to comprehend.

In the following months, I had an encounter with the Angels Xedah, and they imparted to me the teachings of Angelic Spiritual Healing. This meeting was no accident; it was actually a re-connection with a relationship which had happened in a past life.

Once in a past-life regression, I had been able to relive my meeting with Xedah in ancient Egypt. I was the daughter of an Egyptian high official. My father had been close to Pharaoh. In this time, the Pharaohs and high priests were not the illumined Beings that their predecessors had been. They were no longer acting from a place of unconditional love and divine wisdom, as their ancestors had done previously.

It was at this period in history that Xedah manifested physically on the earth. It was an incarnation from the Source, and he came to transmit a message of love and peace so that people would open their hearts and consciousness to God. He told me to transcend the material world and to live with detachment because difficult times were on their way. It's important to remember that at this time Egypt was spiritually decadent and people were drowning in materialism.

At this time, I was a solitary young girl. I did my daily chores. I was not inclined to socialize; instead, I spent a lot of time in meditation. I had developed psychic powers which allowed me to read people's minds and to perceive their true intentions. After having seen so much egoism and materialism, I was driven to seek out a life of solitude.

The presence of Xedah nourished me spiritually. I felt united with him and protected by him. Xedah was my spiritual father. When I heard his talks, I bathed in the peacefulness and unconditional love which emanated from him. Thus the desire to serve the Source was born in me.

Meanwhile, I could tell that certain people were afraid of his teachings and doubted him because they were too attached to their social positions and their possessions. Just before Xedah left the earth plane, I had one last encounter with him. Our imminent separation was causing me great pain. It was a moment of intense sadness for me. My heart was breaking. My face was pressed against his, and I was crying. He caressed my hair tenderly and dried my tears. He told me that this separation was illusory, and that we would always be united, that I had to serve the Source by bringing comfort and love to human beings in the difficult times to come. He told me to continue to spread his teachings and that as a result of my service, I would not feel our separation.

He reminded me that I was a child of God and that God never abandons His children. Since the beginning of time, my soul had chosen to serve the Source. He told me that in a future incarnation we would meet again and I would receive a specific teaching for working with the different bodies of energy which surround human beings, and that this would help heal their souls. After Xedah left, Egypt was destroyed by natural disasters, commonly known as the seven plagues of Egypt. At that time, the Egyptian people were going through a great test and many difficulties. I accomplished the mission of my soul by bringing comfort and love to humans in need and by spreading the teachings of Xedah.

When the time came for me to leave the earth plane, I felt happy and greatly comforted. I felt myself sweetly drawn into the light, and I was welcomed by angels. This past-life regression allowed me to understand that the healing work I was doing was nothing more than a continuation of that which had begun a long time before.

A short time after this past-life regression, I received the teachings of the Angelic Spiritual Healing. While preparing myself to do a series of interventions on someone, I would take a moment to become inwardly focused. I would put myself in a state of readiness and openness and ask Xedah and the angels to help with the healing.

A feeling of well-being and calmness would wash over me. I would feel a golden white light cleaning and purifying my *sushumna*.[1] I became lighter and lighter. At this moment, I saw and felt the angels enter the top of my head. My sushumna was like a crystal cylinder and the angels were positioned on a round platform which had a white railing around the outside of it. The railing was beautifully decorated with finely-worked motifs. Overhead was a lovely roof which looked like a bower. The platform was a luminous, scintillating white color, and it was, in fact, a type of celestial vehicle, supernaturally beautiful. It fit perfectly into my sushumna and descended slowly.

The angels, some standing, others sitting, were situated all around the railing, and they smiled at me, full of joy. Their bodies were made of light and their very real wings looked like white, velvety peacock feathers.

Their presence and their vibration spread throughout my being. It felt like a healing balm, and it filled me with a deep happiness. I had the impression that I had received a gift of divine grace, and I felt myself become one with the angels.

---

[1]The circuit of energy situated along the spinal column allowing the awakening of the Kundalini Energy.

Now, each time I perform an intervention on the subtle bodies of someone, I recall this experience and reconnect with it. Then, immediately, I feel again the powerful vibration of their angelic presence descend upon me, transferring their healing powers.

—*Ninon Prévost*
August, 1995

Prologue

─────────⟨∞⟩─────────

"The healing we're talking about is not a concept, because healing is an act of love, an experience of unconditional love, which permits the elevation of the soul."
— *The Angels Xedah*

*B*ecause your society functions by concepts, healing is put in a little box which creates belief systems such as "healing can only happen through the physical body. If the physical body has not been healed, there has been no healing." We call this conditional healing. If there is a condition, there is no healing. This is a concept of healing. As soon as a condition is placed on an experience, you conceptualize it. The healing we're talking about is not a concept, because healing is an act of love, an experience of unconditional love which permits the elevation of the soul.

We understand that in your society humans identify themselves with their physical form. If a human should look at himself in a mirror and realize he doesn't have the height which is highly regarded in your society, he doesn't love himself. If he doesn't have the right eye color, broad shoulders, or if he doesn't have the waistline that is recognized and valued by your society, then he doesn't love himself. What does this tell you? That the human in your society identifies himself totally with his physical form, and he tries to heal his physical form when he shows signs of illness. However, this is very limited because you are not just a physical form! You know that after death you put a body in the fire or under the ground, or even in the water, so the form is no longer. Where is the soul? Imagine a human who identifies himself with his body. When the time comes for him to leave his body, how can he leave? It's difficult. Imagine an incarnate entity who has obtained an illness: cancer, for example. During his illness, this human believes that healing can only occur on the physical level and he does not believe that he will recover from this illness with this type of healing. How will the soul leave? It's difficult.

The concept of healing that is well-loved and shared by many practitioners in our society is a limited concept, because it is conditional. There is more than just the body. You are, above all, eternal souls, and your soul is sustained by the unconditional. If your soul is sustained or nourished by the conditional, it suffers. And you may ask, "Why is this the case? Why does our soul suffer in the conditional?" This is very simple. The conditional is not the true nature of your soul. Imagine a human who, during his entire life, wanted to be a musician and became an engineer instead because of his parents or as a result of his conditioning. This human would suffer because his true nature is to express himself with music. It's the same thing with the soul. The true nature of your soul is unconditional because the true nature of your soul is the divine source. It doesn't matter whether you believe this or not, it's true. If you possessed the capacity to see the invisible and could truly see all the souls around you, you would see the flame of the holy spirit shining with all its light in each of these souls. A person might be the biggest criminal on earth ever known, and this flame would still exist. Such is the nature of the soul. And this nature is unconditional.

What kind of healing helps the soul? Unconditional healing. You cannot have any other healing. Healers are discovering this experience in themselves. The light that they are channeling while they are healing and the actions of moving their hands are unconditional actions. Their hands of light on the subtle bodies are not within the constraints of a condition. Do you believe that light is conditional? Not at all. If you project a condition upon it, you are blocking the unconditional. Healers are beings who choose to use their channeling and receiving abilities to ignite love in themselves and to transmit it through their hands, their hearts, and their consciousness. In their channeling there is no place for conditions. When they touch different subtle bodies of individuals with their hands of light, they are not contemplating whether the skin is green or the skin is brown, or judging the color of the hair, and they are not acting on the subtle bodies.

Channeling love requires the healers' love. This is why this initiation in healing is an initiation of self-healing. Many forms of healing exist which are called medical: osteopathic and others. Enlarge your consciousness. All healing is spiritual, because all healing dwells in the unconditional. There must be healing of the soul before all else. This does not mean that while one is acting on the subtle bodies the physical body cannot heal itself. But don't place this condition. Leave the light to act. The light knows. The soul knows. The soul knows if its healing is going to manifest in the physical form, or if the healing must manifest in the subtle body, or if it must leave this physical form with the illness and continue the healing on another plane. You don't know. Only the energy of the divine source knows. This requires a total letting go in order to let the divine light act without conditions or restraints. Certainly the ego of a healer wants to be inflated: "I have healed a patient with cancer!" you can say. "Who has healed whom?" we ask. In channeling there no longer exists an "I." You cannot force a soul to heal itself, because the soul is free, and this liberty is what helps the soul in its growth process. The soul possesses the power to choose light or darkness. The soul is free, constantly free. The soul cannot be conditional and carry the divine source.

You do have the inner power to manifest healing in the cells of the physical body, and other forms of healing can also act on the cells of the physical body. However, unconditional healing does not have conditions. Observe humans. Contemplate that for many of them healing is conditional. This is an illusion, a distortion of the manifestation of the ego, a false understanding, because healing is unconditional. It does not require conditions. The human who asks the divine source to heal his physical form, but who does not become healed, questions himself and says to himself, "Am I worse than my neighbor or am I doing less for my physical form that it cannot heal itself like I want it to?" Instead, the human should ask himself, "Should my physical form heal itself?"

Have the humility to ask the unconditional. Have the humility to open yourselves to these teachings. Not only ours, but all of the teachings which transmit the unconditional. Is it not through the unconditional that you can manifest every form of healing? The human who hates his physical form because it does not respond to healing is in an illusion. How can hate heal? How can we heal by hating that part of the body which is unable to heal itself (in the way that the ego wants it to heal)? In healing, there is no place for self-hatred. There is no place for this in the unconditional. For us, you are all—no matter your height, your weight, the length of your hair, the color of your skin, or whether you are male or female—you are all spiritual beings. For us angels, your nature is spiritual. Thus, healing is spiritual because you are spiritual. Such is your profound nature. It could be that you have forgotten it, and this is not important, because every second you can remind yourself that you are divine, even though you may have other judgments about yourself. Often we tell humans that an entity that you judge as the biggest criminal on the planet is *just as divine as the greatest saint on the planet. Healing acts through the criminal as well as through the saint, because healing does not put conditions on anyone. Divine love is without conditions. It is possible for any being to manifest healing. It is possible for any being to channel healing and transmit it.*

"... only love heals."
—The Angels Xedah

Chapter One

Spiritual Angelic Healing

"Ever since the earth has existed, certain angels have had the mission of intervening on all vibratory forms on this planet and adjusting their vibratory and energetic fluids, the prana, which nourishes earthly forms."
—The Angels Xedah

The types of spiritual healing which are practiced in your society work on the subtle bodies as well as the physical body. Spiritual angelic healing works on the subtle bodies. These are composed of the tissue, the core, and a line which, like a river, circulates from top to bottom through the center, not separating it, but embedded in it. The prana circulates in this river. The prana is the divine energy which nourishes everything, including trees and plants, in such a way that the cells of the tissue, for example, stay held together. Some of you may explain this by alchemy. However, alchemy is nourished by divine energy. Prana exists everywhere. Without prana, nothing could exist on your planet. Prana is simply divine love, vibratory fluid. All of the subtle bodies which create an earthly entity's cocoon of light are nourished by the prana and nourish themselves by the river bed which circulates from top to bottom through the core.

What is angelic healing? You may be familiar with certain forms of healing on the subtle bodies. Many beings, both celestial and earthly, act on the core of these subtle bodies, others act on the tissue of these subtle bodies. You will understand these terms better when the anatomy of the subtle bodies is described. The vibrational river circulating in the center of the core is directly related to the chakras. This center, this line, this river, is called the median line. The angels of haling act primarily on this median line and on the energetic fluid called prana which circulates in the river and which nourishes the core of each subtle body.

The goals of spiritual angelic healing are the harmonization of the subtle bodies, the channeling of love and light, and the upliftment of the soul by stimulating and energizing the light which already exists.

This intervention is specific to the Angels of Healing, the Angels Xedah. This does not make this intervention better or worse, although a number of earthly entities have this tendency—originating in the left hemisphere of the brain—to compare rather than to welcome. We would like to say that this form of healing has already existed for a long time within the scale of earthly time. Ever since the earth has existed, certain angels have had the mission of intervening on all vibratory forms on this planet and adjusting their vibratory and energetic fluids, the prana, which nourishes earthly forms.

Chapter Two

The Subtle Bodies

Many spiritual traditions teach that the human being possesses, in addition to his physical body, seven other bodies which surround the physical body. These bodies are etheric, emotional, mental, astral, supra-astral, celestial, and the body of Light.

All of these bodies are connected. They interpenetrate each other, starting with the physical body and extending from it, all maintaining their own frequency. One can visualize these subtle bodies as successive envelopes of light and energy which are interwoven. The physical body does not function on its own. There are the subtle bodies which maintain its equilibrium. Knowledge of these bodies is very important because by knowing how to act on them, one can transform the state of health and spiritual growth of a person. Thus, to guarantee a state of true health, the subtle bodies must be in perfect alignment.

Each body possesses its own tissue, and its individual structure is formed from a sound core. At the center of each core is a longitudinal opening called the median line. This line has a specific thickness and width. The vital energy which is called the energetic fluid, or prana, circulates in this median line. It sustains, in its turn, the energy centers called chakras. These chakras are part of the median line. This fluid helps the good functioning of different bodily systems. It helps assimilation and elimination. Its disequilibrium can lead to the appearance of degenerating illnesses.

We will try to give you a more precise image of these subtle bodies. Each one of these bodies contains both tissue and core. As with a piece of fruit—a peach for example—the pit, or core, is more dense than the fruit, or tissue, which is vaporous. Each core is surrounded by the others in the same fashion as a set of Russian dolls. Thus the core of the astral body includes the core of the mental which includes the core of the emotional, which includes the etheric, which includes the physical. They all have a distinct identity and a distinct vibration, and all of the cores share a substance which is more vaporous: the tissue. The tissue has a vibration which is more global even though each body has its own vibration.

At the center of each core exists a longitudinal opening called the median line which is embedded in the center just like a river in a riverbed, and its fluid flows from the celestial plane to the earthly plane. This river is positioned in front of and behind each core along the line of the chakras. The vital energy called prana (in Sanskrit) circulates in this channel, and this energy nourishes the core, the tissue, and the entire being. You can compare the median line in this configuration to a river with a fluidity more or less rapid, more or less dense, or to a highway which has fissures, unevenness, some hills or big rocks corresponding to the crystallizations of energy in the case of each individual.

The median line takes its source from beyond the three superior chakras or celestial roots above the crown and passes above the line of the physical chakras. The pranic fluidity circulates there like a river, and this river continues all the way to the three chakras under the feet, or the earthly roots, called the inferior chakras. The pranic fluidity originates in the celestial planes and roots itself in the earthly planes in front of and behind the body. On this line of chakras rests the median line, the river receiving the pranic fluidity, flowing from top to bottom. The same thing in the back: you have this river which also flows from top to bottom.

This river in vibrationally healthy humans can vary from a width of 5 to 8 centimeters (or 2 1/2 to 3 inches). The width of this line is not necessarily different for a man or a woman, but you can see a difference in the pranic fluidity. In women the pranic fluidity is sometimes much more subtle than in men where the fluidity is more active and easy to locate. This is directly associated with their respective capacity. The incarnate soul which has chosen a woman's body has chosen to be more sensitive, more receptive to all vibrational forms, and you can see this in the median line. We are not saying that it is a direct equation. However, the median line in a woman has a softer and more receptive fluidity than a man whose fluidity is less refined, less subtle. The bodies, the receptivity, the hormonal cycles in a woman, make her more receptive and more sensitive. The depth of this median line is approximately 4-5 centimeters (or 2-2 1/2 inches). The line is embedded in the core, and this line becomes the river bed. The pranic fluidity is the water feeding the core. Surrounding this core is the tissue.

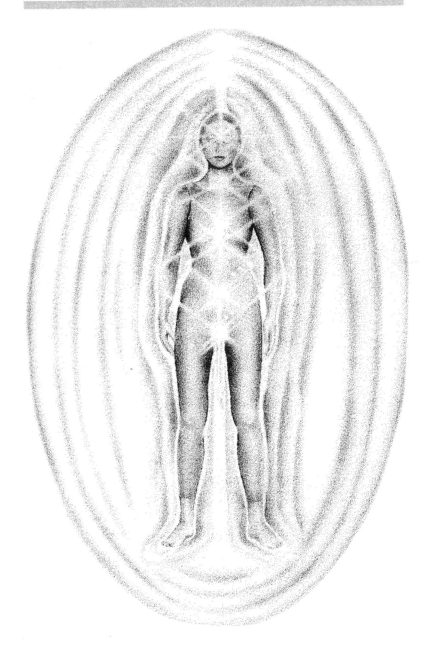

Subtle Bodies

Subtle Bodies (from the side)

The Body Zero: The Physical Body

The body zero is the physical body: dense, but at the same time vibrational. So vibrational that healers can penetrate the physical body with their hands of light, such as the Philippine healers. This shows you that the destiny of the physical body can be changed by the manipulation of light energy. If the hands of light successfully dematerialize the physical body, the physical hands can penetrate. The physical body is, thus, vibrational.

The Earthly Bodies

The subtle bodies known as earthly: the etheric body, the emotional body, and the mental body are the bodies directly associated with this incarnation, just like the physical body. The earthly bodies are very easy to recognize. They are more dense than the others in the core and also in the median line.

The First Body: The Etheric Body

The first body is the etheric body, which envelopes the physical body totally. It is the duplicate, the double of the physical body. Sensitive beings, when they touch the etheric body, can feel there pains and the uneasiness which have become lodged in the physical body, because the etheric body is affected before the physical body. The physical body is the last body to be affected by symptoms of illness, by disequilibrium. The language of the etheric is < <I am sick. I am uneasy. I have no energy. > >

The subtle etheric body, on the part of most vibrationally healthy beings, is around 30 centimeters or 12 inches above the physical form. However, in certain humans you are going to find it closer to the physical body. If it is very close, or tightly against the physical form, the human certainly has difficulties. This signifies that the body cannot breathe: not only the physical, but also the etheric body. If the etheric body has collapsed onto the *physical, the physical suffers manifestations in the cells or internal organs. This is what you can call an illness. When in the presence of a spiritual master, beings who have meditated, entities who channel through a medium, or beings who have received hours of teaching, sometimes the etheric body might become swollen.*

Thus the etheric is the double of the physical and has for a goal the protection of the physical form. When the healer touches the median line of the etheric body, it may feel like the hands are touching the pains that the physical body is not experiencing or has already experienced.

The etheric body is a copy conforming to the physical body on a more subtle plane. It faithfully reflects the state of health. In fact, the two bodies are so closely inter-related that it is difficult to disassociate them except in the case of shock, an accident, or serious trauma.

By absorbing the effects coming from the other bodies— before affecting the physical body—the etheric body, which remains flexible as a way to maintain equilibrium between the two, serves as a filter, as a last defense. But if it happens to become weak, illnesses and problems of a karmic order have the tendency to penetrate into the physical body.

The Second Body: The Emotional Body

The emotional body uses another language entirely. It is the second subtle earthly body. It possesses all the emotions which the earthly entity has experienced since its birth, or even before birth, until now. And it may also possess emotions experienced in other lives which are affecting this present one. When reading this body, not only will you find there blockages which prevent the pranic fluidity, but you may also read emotions such as anger, sadness, disappointment, rage, a great wound in the heart, and joy. They can come from this existence, just as they can come from other existence's. It is very easy to recognize this, because you will find these emotions in the astral body, also, if they've come from previous lives. Thus these crystallized emotions found in the emotional body influence the etheric body and create blockages in the etheric as well as the physical body.

If one is healthy, the distance separating the etheric from the emotional body will be a little less than that which separates the etheric from the physical. If it is sick, it can be flattened or crushed onto the adjacent body. The emotional body is the body where are lodged all the emotions experienced by this entity during this lifetime, as well as the emotions which come from past lives—because the emotional body receives information from the astral body. So, imagine an earthly entity who, during this incarnation, experienced a feeling of permanent anger which comes from a past life. This goes largely beyond memory, even of this present life. You are going to read this emotion in the emotional body. It will be lodged there, because the being experienced it during this life.

The emotional body is the form in which the human being feels all his emotions, sensations, and sentiments. It is equally the seat of desires, passions, attractions, repulsions, and character traits upon which reason often has little impact. It is there, equally, that are accumulated all the pains, joys, aspirations, hopes, fears and sources of anxiety related not only to this present incarnation, but also to past lives. For someone who can see the emotional body, it appears as a field of energy which is tinted by the colors of different felt emotions. The perturbations of the emotional body can destabilize the different systems of the physical body, and if all the emotional baggage is not decrystallized, there is a risk of affecting and even suffocating the life force.

The Third Body: The Mental Body

The third body is the mental body. It possesses all the beliefs and all the systems of belief which the entity has chosen to *experience in this incarnation, as well as, the conditioning of social, familial and even planetary beliefs. When you diagnose the median line of the mental body, you are going to read there the configurations which are blocking it. But, also, you are going to read, < < I am not enough. I am not loved enough. I am not able to love. I am afraid of men. I am closed to love, to God. God is angry at me. > > And all other forms of beliefs. There are so many! These beliefs may be coming from the experience of the soul in this incarnation, but they can also be influenced by the astral body which is just above the mental body; thus they can influence the mental body. You will know that these beliefs have come from past lives if you find them also in the astral body.*

The mental body transports all forms of vibrational thoughts from different systems of beliefs which come from this lifetime or which have been influenced by other lifetimes.

The mental body which corresponds to the psyche is the third form where the profound and anchored beliefs are accumulated: habits of thoughts, impressions and resistances, notably the resistance to want to elevate one's consciousness.

This body is also the subtle seat of conscious and unconscious thought. An examination of this body allows us to detect the patterns of thought which often resurface from infancy and which are responsible for mental and emotional disequilibrium. The adult who wishes to become conscious of these patterns of thought may be able to recognize them and transform them.

The Fourth Body: The Astral Body

The astral body appears on the astral plane. The astral plane is close to the earthly plane, however it is not an earthly plane. Among other things, time does not exist. If a subject is led through his past lives which exist at the same time as this, it's possible that the subject will connect with a life from the 18th century, even the 4th century, even before Christ. There is no longer a logic of time, because we are no longer on the earthly plane. The median line and the core of the astral body are a door opening into the astral plane. This is why it is suggested that the healer who touches this body be well-grounded, because he can lose his ground. The astral body does not belong to the earth. While treating the astral body, the healer can read all the past lives of the individual.

The astral body is the door opening to the dimension of the astral where time does not exist and where all the lives are being lived at the same time as this one. When the healer places his hands on the median line of the astral, he observes that it is much larger than the others, or seems to be slipping away from under his hands. The astral plane is a plane where one can meet wandering souls, where one can read all the past lives, where one can meet up with karmic memories. The astral body of each one of these entities is lodged in the astral plane and is also lodged in the astral of the planet.

The astral body is a transition point between the earthly and celestial bodies. All the karmic memories and impressions of past lives are accumulated there. These vibrating memories start in the astral body and influence us constantly. We call these vibrating memories < < karmic energies. > > Although the soul possesses his energy and his own immutable vibration, the karma of the individual influences its expression. Intervention on this body permits a soul to be freed from the impressions of the past. It permits the soul to be able to understand and transform these impressions so that he can become conscious of the mission that he has chosen.

The Celestial Bodies

Beyond the earthly and astral bodies exist three other bodies which transcend the earthly plane: the supra-astral body, the celestial body, and the body of Light.

The Fifth Body: The Supra-astral Body

The fifth body is the supra-astral or the etheric of the astral, the duplicate of the astral. It is a buffer of protection between the astral planes and the celestial planes, not allowing the possibility of incompatible energies to penetrate the celestial plane.

The fifth body does not allow the events occurring in the astral body to touch the celestial body. It protects like the etheric protects the physical body. It is part of the plane that we are going to call the highest astral.

The supra-astral body is the body which receives the highest qualities of unconditional love, of compassion and detachment.

The Sixth Body: The Celestial Body

The sixth body is the celestial body. When you touch it, you can see the guides and guardian angels of this entity. The guardian angels, the healing angels, and the angels of communication are seated there very comfortably. Certain healers speak with these guides while touching this body. Touching this body raises vibrations. This body is a sacred body. The celestial body is the body in which can be found all the entities of light, the guides, and highly evolved souls who can help you in your incarnation. Thus the celestial body permits communication with these celestial planes. The celestial body is a body of love.

The celestial body permits an individual to feel the vibrations from the celestial plane and to communicate with the guides of light, spiritual masters, angels, and archangels of healing.

The Seventh Body: The Body Of Light

The seventh body is the vehicle of the soul when it leaves the earthly plane. The soul ascends with its body of light; it takes its seventh body and leaves. This body envelopes all of the other bodies; it protects them and nourishes them with the energy of the celestial planes. However, the seventh body is not the last body, because beyond it exists again seven other bodies, and again seven others and so on until infinity. In this sense you are more vast than you ever believed. These bodies belong to the planes which you visit and which you will utilize when you leave the earthly plane. They serve the soul in certain passages of evolution in the beyond. The soul always travels—we're not speaking of astral travels—with its body of light when it finally leaves this planet. The seven first bodies are the vehicles responsible for evolution on the earthly plane.

The body of light is the body of the Source, the body utilized by the soul to travel in the spaces beyond time, beyond light. This is why we call it the body associated with the plane of the Source. When the guides come to influence the soul, to guide it, they are not in the body of light. They are in the celestial body. The body of light must stay totally free and only influenced by very high planes of light. The body of light is the soul's vehicle of light.

The body of light is in a plane of light and is nourished by this plane, just as the astral body is in the astral plane and is nourished by this plane. The soul uses the energy from the plane of light when it leaves with its body of light, which allows it to then travel to different planes of consciousness. When the soul travels like this, his essence helps the propulsion of this body of light. Thus the soul must be very evolved, very transformed, to travel in the plane of light and to serve the Source there.

The plane of light is difficult to describe in human terms. We the angels have access to the plane of light. As entities or sparks of the Source, we serve the Source. Therefore, we utilize this plane to serve the Source. However, it is not through this plane that we have access to serve the souls on the earth. To serve the souls on the earth, to serve humans, we use the celestial plane. And so do other guides, masters and entities.

The seventh body or body of light is the highest plane and permits the soul to communicate directly with the Source itself. Nevertheless, the individual is hardly even conscious of this constant communication at the subtle level because the accumulation of his karmic baggage impedes the light of these higher planes to penetrate his physical form.

Thus, it is in the fifth body where the feelings of self-hatred and indignity can manifest and read there like blockages on the median line. In the sixth it is the lack of opening, the lack of faith in the presence and authenticity of guides and spiritual masters which create blockages. In the seventh, it is the feeling of separation from the Source which blocks the experience of union.

The spiritual healer places himself in a state of total communion with the Source and becomes a pure channel to transmit energy and unconditional love to the supra-astral body, to transmit the energy of universal knowledge to the celestial body, and to transmit divine energy to the body of light. This will have the effect of charging them with energy, of awakening them, of stimulating them, and of making them vibrate at a higher frequency.

The Function Of The Subtle Bodies In Out-Of-Body Travel

These very subtle bodies are the constant vehicle of your soul. When you travel in the astral plane, you constantly have the supra-astral body, the celestial body, and the body of light as layers to protect you.

The bodies never become separate. The bodies are very strongly connected. However, imagine that an entity decides to embark on an astral voyage. His physical form is resting. The etheric serves as protection, the same with the mental and emotional bodies. The astral body opens itself. The median line equally must open itself so that the being and his consciousness can travel in the astral.

This is why many individuals have said, upon coming back from astral voyages, that they've had difficulty re-entering their physical forms. In order to do this, all the bodies must be able to adjust themselves in order to make it back from their voyage to the astral. When the soul comes back, it must re-penetrate all the layers of the physical body. Otherwise this creates a profound disequilibrium. These bodies exist for very specific reasons of protection. They help the entity remain autonomous.

If you know beings who travel in the astral just for the pleasure of doing it, it's very important to check if all their bodies have been well positioned. Journeys to the astral plane are only suggested if they are done as research, because often these beings know how to leave but do not return well and have difficulty to reinhabit all the bodies. These bodies which are not well reinhabited lack nourishment. It is very important that the soul completely reinhabits the physical form because the soul creates nourishment. The more that the soul lives in the form, the more the bodies will stay healthy. The more that you live in your physical form, the more you can evolve without harming the good health of all your subtle bodies.

Chapter Three

The Development Of A Child's Subtle Bodies

*U*sually the bodies of a newborn are in vibrational form and not completely formed. This little being begins to breathe by himself, nourishing himself by the prana for the first time alone.

The physical body is nourished both by the breath and by the prana: thoracic respiration as well as cellular respiration. You are not conscious of cellular respiration, but it is as important as breathing. The pranic nourishment helps formation of the bodies which are the covering and support of the physical body. This is why a newborn cannot live by himself and must be close to the bodies of other adults and thus be nourished by the physical forms of his adult parents so that his own physical layers can be formed.

You may observe that certain children at the age of two or three years have already formed their small structural layers. If their bodies are formed, they have the capacity to absorb spiritual nourishment for their physical body. Certain children are more slow in this development, and this also depends on the parents and the incarnation that they have chosen. If the infant is constantly hit, if he is never embraced or protected, this does not help the formation of these bodies. The more that the bodies are formed, the more the soul is installed in the physical body.

When a child is born—if this soul has lived many lives already—it's possible that the bodies are already formed or semi-formed. In this case, you are in the presence of a being who will be a master on your planet. His power is such that, as soon as the umbilical cord has been cut, already the subtle bodies will be formed in a rhythm much faster than that of other souls. Thus, Avatars[1] never need a natural mother; however, they have one out of respect for your society. As soon as they are born they have all their layers and can, from the very beginning, touch and heal.

You as souls have chosen an earthly incarnation. There are many energies circulating on the earth. On this planet earth the physical form inhabited by a soul is called human. The human has accepted that the soul will be born in this way: as a small child. He has accepted to undergo the growth process of physical and psychic forms as is expected on the planet earth.

On other planets, this is not seen in the same fashion. However, as souls, you have chosen this earth. You have chosen in this moment on your planet earth, that a child will be small. The little one nourishes itself with the vibrational bodies of its parents in order to build its own bodies and to strengthen the chakras. Thus the child is dependent on the vibrational energy of its parents until the subtle bodies have been completely formed. We call it spiritual maturity when the child can detach himself from his parents and live off of his own bodies.

In this moment on this planet, spiritual maturity occurs at the approximate age of 5, 6, or 7 years old. Psychic maturity is not completely developed at this time. It's not possible. If you were on another planet and your soul was incarnated in a different form, the process would not be the same. It is very important that you realize that this is true of the planet earth: the process of

---

[1]Avatar: Born master. Being who is realized and divine from the moment of birth.

psychic maturity is experienced later than the process of spiritual maturity.

Spiritual maturity helps the child to develop the chakras and his bodies. This gives him a basis which will permit him to become psychically mature with the help of his society and his actual parental conditions. In ideal conditions, this maturation will be completed during the period of adolescence. This period also corresponds to a burst of spiritual growth.

The hormonal releases that begin for you on this planet approximately at adolescence must be experienced with a developed spiritual maturity. Can you imagine some subtle bodies not formed, not solid, and suddenly there are glands which set off hormonal releases creating a large amount of activity at the level of the chakras? This would be very harmful.

When we speak about spiritual maturity, we're speaking about the development of the subtle bodies. At the age of 5, 6, or 7 years old the child, in the majority of cases on your planet, has his bodies already formed. That is, if he has not experienced a profound trauma, a profound abandonment, and if the child has not grown up alone. If a child has grown up alone in nature, for example, he would receive the energy of the animal who has taken care of him. However, this would not help and adequate formation of his bodies. The child builds his bodies with the nourishment and support of the bodies of his parents or their substitutes.

Ideally, the psychic maturity must already be in process at the period of adolescence when the child begins to fly with his own wings. At this time there is a burst of growth due to hormonal movement which helps spiritual maturity. It is initiation. A true initiation. We're speaking of the ideal situations which should be experienced on your planet.

However, for this hormonal activity to be like an initiation, all the bodies must be formed and in place. This dramatic change is necessary in order for the child to attain a psychic liberation from his parents. This is a true initiation. In your society this initiation has become very distorted. This is why most adolescents are totally dragged down by the unconscious collective of other adolescents and the unconscious collective of the planet: they don't have a psychic and spiritual solidity.

Certain ones of them suffer from great deficiencies in their spiritual anatomy when this burst of growth occurs. This growth spurt does not necessarily wait until all the bodies have been formed, well in place, and very solid. This growth spurt may come in such a way that the children cannot absorb the initiative shock. These are the ones who want to leave the planet because their souls do not wish to live any longer.

This creates a distortion: the hormonal activity becomes channeled in a violent and cruel way and can even provoke that which we call insanity. In this sense, adolescents are very vulnerable; every warrior must go through initiations which test their vulnerability. Not having the social or familial support necessary for their growth, however, these adolescents are totally affected by the astral forces, by the dark forces, or by the unconscious collective. This creates another distortion which is evident in your society. When there's a lack of human presence and support, certain adolescents seek an artificial paradise through the use of alcohol, drugs or other things. These dependencies accompany the hormonal and spiritual initiation which is experienced by these beings.

These beings are preparing themselves for the adult phase, which should be a phase of total creativity and expansion of the divine essence. This is not the case, and your society has chosen this—we are offering you a mirror. Your society holds all its beliefs in a box and imposes them on these adolescents who are preparing themselves to become individuals and independent. Individuality is thus experienced in a prison created by a series of social conditioning and beliefs. You have chosen this. This is

*what is experienced at this moment on your planet. However, it
is a total distortion.*

*The child nourishes himself from the energy of his parents.
He breathes their energy. When a child is in the arms of his
parent, he is influenced by his energetic field because he does not
have his subtle bodies formed. He is totally enveloped by the
subtle bodies of his parents and is nourished by them. He takes in
their energy. Have you noticed all the little ones when they're
following their parents? They are constantly searching for that
energetic field. When they're just getting ready to leave, already
they're rushing back. They leave and they come back. Isn't there
this movement? This is a sign that these small bodies are just
beginning to be developed. However, they still need to reach out
and draw from the energy of their parent. This is why, if the
parent does not maintain a good healthy vibrational energy, he
becomes empty, because he's giving his vital energy to his child.*

*Because a child's subtle bodies have no armor and no mass
crystallizations, the child is very receptive, and thus more
vulnerable. The communication with the parent is direct. Very
direct. Is the parent listening?*

In my practice I received a few children and adolescents.
It is always a very enriching experience for me to be able to
contribute to their development and accompany them on
the path of discovering the light. In the process of these
meetings, I noticed that the communication with the souls
of these young beings was generally much easier than it was
with adults. This can be explained by the fact that the bodies
are not yet completely developed, and they are not yet filled
with impressions caused by the experiences of this present
life. It is also obvious that the familial context can either
favor or hinder this communication.

Sometimes it happens that a soul can be incarnated,
and his development can profit from either favorable or

unfavorable circumstances. For example, one day I treated a woman who was seven months pregnant. During this intervention I felt the vibrations of the soul of this child that she was carrying. This child was happy to receive these healing energies. Intuitively I understood that this child had come to liberate himself from feelings of abandonment because this woman who was carrying him had been his mother in a past life, and she had left him. They had come together again to harmonize their relationship. After his birth, this child became receptive to spirituality and is very sensitive to healing energies.

One day I received a very depressed adolescent at my office. After the separation of his parents, he lived with his father who he considered his role model. The father drank alcohol and took tranquilizers, suffered from depression, and obviously was not very happy. All of this ended by his death. The child had to return to live with his mother. He had difficulty integrating himself in this new home, this new situation, and he had conflicts with his mother. This adolescent was becoming more and more like his father. He took alcohol and drugs to end his discomfort. His mother, in order to help him surmount these difficulties, suggested he come and see me.

At his examination, I noticed that his etheric body was very close to his physical body, and that his median line was thin and his energetic fluidity was slow. This was illustrated by a lack of energy. There were parasites which had hampered the sushumna, so that there was a gap in the energetic fluidity corresponding to some digestive problems, and this gap also distressed the plexus chakra and hara chakra.

The emotional body was stained by a dark gray, and the median line was also very thin. This body was folded up on itself, showing a great repression or denial of emotions. The gap in the plexus and hara was filled with feelings of fear.

The mental body was heavy. The median line here was very narrow which showed he had a certain mental rigidity. The thought forms had become like parasites in this body.

In the astral body, I felt a strong influence of his deceased father, thus, some very strong feelings of anguish and fear. At this moment, the soul of the adolescent revealed to me that it had been incarnated only to liberate himself from these fears and to proceed on the path.

After two treatments the adolescent told me he no longer felt like taking alcohol or drugs anymore and that he really wanted to follow this path which he had already begun, with the goal of understanding why he had chosen to have these experiences in this life. Taking an equal interest in the health of his body, he registered in a physical fitness center and undertook modifications in his diet.

Another time a father brought his child of nine years to see me. This child suffered from violent migraines each time he practiced a physical contact sport. The medical tests that he had sustained bad not shown any serious health problem.

During my examination of him, I noticed that the median line of his etheric body was very large, like that of a healer. His energetic fluid gave off a lot of heat in the cervical region. I had many visions of his past lives where, as a healer, he had received hits on his head, which had sometimes even lead to his death. Certain meridians were still like this in this present life, and they had retained this fragility. Each time that he experienced a collision with another child, these migraines would be triggered. Even his sense of inner equilibrium would be affected.

At the level of his emotional body, I felt that this child feared combat. And, what's more, he had a great admiration for his father and was constantly trying to please him. This desire, which on some level disturbed him, permitted him unconsciously to escape from his fears. It is obvious at this point that he is still too young to be conscious of and to confront this desire to please his father, but later in his life he will have to work at liberating himself from this desire.

The influence of his father was, again, very noticeable at the level of his mental body. The child had not sufficiently developed his own system of beliefs. The karmic relationship uniting these two was very strong because there had been a number of lives in which these two were both warriors.

When I read his astral body, the information I received from his soul told me that this being must now free himself from his karma by becoming a peaceful warrior, by learning to let go, by turning toward milder physical disciplines. After a few more treatments, his migraines diminished in intensity, but he had to be prudent and stop his physically violent sports.

Chapter Four

The Chakras

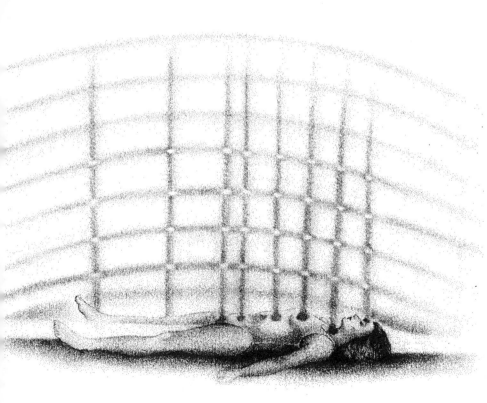

All of the meridian lines are directly connected to the chakras of the subtle bodies that you touch. Thus, if you touch the meridian line of the emotional body and you pass to the level of the region of the solar plexus, you also touch the radiance of the chakra of the heart and of the solar plexus in the emotional body. Because the chakras radiate, spread out, and join at the different subtle bodies, there is not a separation. This helps the healers read the configurations better and creates a necessary link between the different crystallizations of energy and their location on the median lines. There are many crystallizations of energy which can hinder the free flow of prana.

The bodies called earthly, etheric, emotional, and mental are connected to the earthly chakras: the base, the hara, and the solar plexus. However, the energy of the chakra of the heart belongs to all of the earthly bodies above-mentioned. When the chakra of the heart is opened, there is a direct association between the heart and the supra-astral body, and the same thing with the consciousness chakra. When it is opened, it is associated directly with the celestial body. It all depends on the level of consciousness of the soul.

On the astral plane one can find all of the chakras because all of the lives exist in the astral plane, and if one life had been very high in vibrational quality, you will find the crown energy there or the other superior chakras: the throat or the consciousness, for example. When we speak about the relation of the chakras with the median lines, we mean that you find the influence of all the chakras on the median lines.

The Base

The base chakra holds the roots of all the other chakras which are equally important, such as the hips, the knees, the ankles, and the feet. The base chakra is a reservoir of vital or spiritual energy which comes from nature, or from the soul in its physical form. This energy of life, this spiritual energy, this sexual energy is natural to the incarnation.

This chakra is a reservoir of love like all the other chakras. It is very important for the life energy of the soul inhabiting a physical form. Its position creates the relationship between the earth and the soul living in this physical form. Of the six other major chakras, the base chakra is the one closest to the earth. Thus, through this chakra the entity establishes his relationship with mother earth which nourishes it, transports it, and sustains it, and on which and in which it evolves during all its years and even centuries. The relation of the earth with all of the base chakras of all humans is very intimate, very important.

When the base chakra is opened, the entity has the force and the solidity of matter and carries love. With the help of this chakra and all the other chakras, the entity can totally fill his physical life with love. Therefore, the energy which is in the reservoir of the base chakra must be used unconditionally and healthily without distortion or compulsion, without under-utilization or over-utilization, without judgments or conditions.

When the roots are cut, the human does not know how to respond to his own vital needs: does not know how to nourish himself when he's hungry, does not know how to drink when he's thirsty, does not how to eliminate when his body needs to. He doesn't even know how to recognize the natural movements of life.

The more the base chakras of your planet and of the humans who live upon it are cut from their vitality and their earthly roots, and, thus, from the celestial roots, the more your planet becomes very vulnerable and easily attacked because it has lost its natural impulse. It has even lost its own sense, its spiritual function.

The expression of the base chakra can be seen in all beings who can dance in their physicality during their daily lives. We are using dancing as a symbolic image. You can be paralyzed and it's still possible to dance in the energy of matter, to spiritualize all that you touch, to elevate matter by the energy of love because matter is love and not far from God. God is everywhere. The Source is in all that is material and non-material.

Those who can manipulate matter healthily are those whose base chakra is harmonized. Matter is there to serve you. Matter in itself waits for you to use it. This planet waits to be used in its essence. All of the chakras of the hips, the knees, the ankles and the feet wait for the permission to extract nourishment from the earth and to transmit celestial nourishment to the earth. The chakra that permits this exchange is the base chakra.

In the base are the vital needs. These vital needs are as spiritual as the crown chakra because you are spiritual beings. The more you respect life, the more you permit life to be. The more you respect your choice of this incarnation, the more you permit this incarnation to be. The more you respect matter, the more you permit matter to be. It is as easy to respect matter as it is for a flower to blossom, and this permits matter to serve you in your path of evolution.

Your base chakra belongs to your essence. You are the master of it. Your base chakra is a jewel. Utilize its energy to nourish you, to uplift you, to help you transcend matter.

The Hara

The hara chakra, just as the base, transports vital energy, but there are some differences. The base is the reservoir of sexual energy and the energy of life. And with all its strength it connects the roots of the earth to the celestial roots of heaven.

The hara is the reservoir of vital energy; however, this energy has become gradually more refined than the base chakra. The function of the love energy of the hara is power in all its purity, grandeur, and force. Unconditional power.

The hara has roots which are much longer than those of the base and which are more refined than those of the base. We're attempting to find strong, concrete terms to describe pure power, this force of life connected with action in the non-action. This planet and many other planets have on it humans who have a distortion of the hara. There are many societies which have belief systems on the subject of power.

The force of the hara, the pure force or strength of the hara, is unwavering. This force of life is a warrior force in which the weapon is the energy of life, the energy of love, the energy of welcoming all that is simple. The force of the hara is not rigid. It is a supple, war-like force; however, it is steadfast.

The flexibility of the power requires humility. The warrior force of the hara is a humble force, totally humble. The hara is humble: neither limp nor rigid, because true power is in humility. In real humility, war-like force can be expressed. We're choosing these earthly terms even though this may create in your mind a contradiction: force, humility, war-like force, humble force. Is it possible that force can be humble? Certainly, because it is unconditional. The expression of pure power is in right action. The hara is the center of action. Not acting just to act and, by acting, forgetting how to be. We're speaking of pure action, of action in the non-action, of stability in flexibility, of force in humility, of the warrior power. You cannot imagine the necessity and the great need for all beings on the earth to possess a flexible hara. Strong and humble. The humble power is very powerful. Not the conditional power of your society. Not the power of your belief systems, but the power like the rising sun. This power is indestructible because it is unconditional.

Let us repeat. The hara is in a very strategic place. It is the second chakra related to the earth and permits right action in the physical as well as in the celestial roots. Thus, a flexible hara does not let itself get disturbed by the ocean of emotions, does not let itself become invaded. Because the hara is flexible it nourishes itself from the energy of the rising sun. This chakra is very important. It is constantly associated with the heart. You could call the hara the heart of action, the heart of the inferior chakras. That's how important it is.

The Plexus

The plexus is calm. The plexus is filled with love. The plexus is a sun. The plexus is the seat, the center, the reservoir of emotions, and emotions are part of the movement of life. This is why sometimes in the reservoir of the plexus there is mobility throughout storms and calm. Emotions are the movement of life.

The life of the plexus, the energy which is situated there, is part of the movement of life. Thus, the emotions are life. Attempting to deny them is attempting to deny yourself, denying that you are earthly. By attempting to deny that you are earthly, that you live in eternal movement, you block the respiration of the sun, you block the respiration of the plexus. In the plexus there is movement. Do not deny this movement. To deny this movement is to deny life.

It is very important to be conscious of the beliefs which affect your relationship with the energy of your plexus. Because if you observe the natural movement of life, life circulates. In life, there is no stagnation, thus, the natural movement of the emotions is a circulation of hormonal energy because the emotions express themselves through the hormonal discharge.

In addition, this center of vital energy is a door of receptivity like all of the chakras. However, this center, in its primary function, is a sun radiating all of its strength and its golden rays, inside and outside. This is the plexus in all its strength, and the plexus, this sun, is well-placed in the center where it radiates love and acceptance, total acceptance of the interior and exterior. However, if this sun is clouded or shaded, if this sun is destroyed, *if the sun is sinking, if the sun has become a point of brilliant and blazing flame, the relationship with the exterior will be disturbed. The plexus refines action. The plexus is related to the action of the hara. The plexus expresses action by communication and that is why it is directly connected with the throat chakra which is the chakra of expression. If the plexus is love, the receptivity of another will be unconditional. If the plexus is hate, it becomes blocked and fixed in the same repetitive movement, and this will be the communication. If the plexus is blocked in sadness, this will be the communication. The plexus is the center of the movement of life, which are the emotions. When the emotions are allowed to be, they are like suns, because they are the expressions of your incarnation.*

The Heart

In the heart chakra, the deepest part of the chakra, is lodged a reservoir, a shaft of love. The chakra of the heart holds unconditional life inside it. Just as the base chakra naturally holds sexual energy and life energy and spiritual energy, just as the hara naturally holds the energy of right action, and just as the plexus carries the midday sun, the heart naturally holds unconditional love.

In the heart you very naturally find unconditional love. You are in your very nature profoundly spiritual beings, and in your physical form you carry the soul, the divine essence. The nourishment of this essence and that which it creates is simply unconditional love. You know because you have felt it. Unconditional love is found in all of the chakras because all of the chakras are nourished and nourish themselves by the prana which contains unconditional love, but also by the natural energy which exists in you, the life energy, the sexual energy, that is the Kundalini. This Kundalini is the energy of love.

The heart chakra is in a very strategic place. The heart chakra is the central point of all the chakras, and just as a cross, it unites the celestial plane with the earthly plane. The junction of these planes cannot be made without going through the energy of love.

This is why the sole and unique path of the union and fusion of the celestial and earthly is through the energy of the heart. All masters know this. Such is the experience of a master: unconditional love. This energy itself transcends everything, and this transcendental power is based in the chakra of your heart. This is why when the heart experiences total unconditional love, it makes peace with all the suffering that your planet holds. The heart is a living laboratory of transcendence, and thus, when the heart nourishes itself totally on unconditional love, it acts like a place of transcendence for all that is not love, holding in the heart < <non-love> > in order to be able to transcend it. Non-love is the suffering which exists on your planet. This is why we repeat: the more the owner of the heart chakra opens his heart, the more he feels suffering. This is neither good nor bad; this is natural, because this is the transcendent power of the heart chakra.

Your souls are free, and unconditional love is free of all conditions. For you to be able to experience your essence, you must experience liberty, and your liberty is without conditions, without social conditions, familial conditions or personal conditions. This does not mean that you are free from all forms of responsibility. This does not mean that you should not fulfill your incarnation. The freedom of which we're speaking is this movement that is not an uprooted or ungrounded freedom. This freedom is an expression of flexibility and of humility.

The Throat

The throat chakra is the chakra of the golden word. Just as in the plexus the emotions are golden, in the throat, words are golden. Because the master's heart chakra is united with his consciousness chakra, his words are golden. These words come from the divine Source, transport a Christ-like vibration, transport a ray of gold, and communicate love totally.

When the throat is in harmony with the heart and the consciousness chakra which are united, they create the intention of love. The throat harmonizes itself, purifies itself and cleanses itself to transmit a sole and unique word which is the Golden Word: the word of love. Thus, these words vibrate with love. These words are fair. They are exactly the right words to transmit the message, the information.

The throat chakra is very well situated between the energy of the heart and the consciousness. The throat chakra is an energy of high communication. It is the chakra used to express the upliftment of consciousness. Certainly this chakra may be utilized for all purposes, including destruction; it can be used to create a state spreading fear and panic, for a state dragging others into submissive action. It is very easy to recognize and to do a reading of the throat chakra.

The golden word is not only a word of teaching; be careful about the illusion of this. The golden word is a word of love. Teaching, the real teaching, is in daily life, in each second of the present moment. It is not only before a crowd, it is in our relation with a dog, a cat, a bird, nature, the dear beings who surround us. Such is the golden word, and this same word can be as easily transmitted to a crowd as to one sole entity, and it carries the same vibration because the golden word is unconditional. It is as unconditional as the wind.

The Consciousness

The consciousness is the divine reservoir. The seat of the divine source. All of your chakras hold this divine essence. All of your chakras hold love. However, the function of the consciousness chakra is a recognition of the divine, and altered perception, a *second vision. We are not speaking about clairvoyance. We are speaking about the capacity to heighten vision to its proper reality, and this is the function of the consciousness.*

The function of the consciousness chakra is upliftment. The consciousness chakra is very important, like all the other chakras. Its location is very strategic because it is just before the crown, and the crown is the door leading to the celestial realms. Thus, if there has not been an elevation, you are not going to be able to use this door. Certain of you can take this door if you cut yourself off from all of the other chakras, but there will be no return.

The hara, the heart, and the consciousness are the reservoirs of power which maintain and nourish life. The consciousness chakra nourishes itself directly from the celestial realms. The consciousness chakra also nourishes itself by the Kundalini. Because there is no separation between the chakras, it can nourish itself from the energy of the base which circulates in the sushumna. The consciousness chakra—due to its location just beneath the celestial door (or crown chakra)—can nourish itself by the celestial energy.

Thus, in the consciousness chakra rests the divine energy itself, rests divine grace, rests upliftment. Just as the heart is a factory, a living laboratory or transcendence, the consciousness is a laboratory also alive with transcendence.

The consciousness is golden. The vibrational potential of this chakra is upliftment, however, upliftment by purification. With this chakra you present everything to the Source, in other words, everything that you have raised through all of your other chakras. Thus, it distills, purifies, and uplifts.

The consciousness discerns. The consciousness does not sleep. The consciousness is awakened. Imagine a peaceful warrior: his consciousness is constantly ready and his hara is constantly ready and his heart is constantly ready; his consciousness is constantly present. Thus, the master is never surprised by darkness, because he is constantly vigilant, receptive, and in an elevated state.

The Crown

When the consciousness chakra and the crown chakra become one, the entity who experiences this process experiences a total change in his own reality and perception. The crown chakra is a door opening to the other planes of consciousness. The consciousness chakra holds the celestial roots of the crown chakra. Because these celestial roots are in the consciousness chakra, an earthly entity can experience the celestial realms. And this entity can receive communication from guides and other beings of light; can locate sacred places on the planet; can read the vibrational doors to the other planes of consciousness on the planet earth; and can let himself be guided to the best time and place to hold meetings which will purify the earth and elevate consciousness. The entity whose consciousness and crown chakra have become one is able to help locate sacred places and find their vibrational power, thereby aiding the earth to evolve and to guide other humans in their upliftment of consciousness.

Follow the path. Continue on this path which is to uplift the consciousness of your planet, to guide humans to recognize their divinity and to uplift their consciousness. Recognize the importance of all the vibrational centers called chakras, and learn the function of these chakras. Help humans to become grounded in the celestial roots as well as the earthly roots.

Chapter Five

Configurations: Obstacles Of The Pranic Fluidity

The principle goal of spiritual angelic healing is to free the soul from the many obstacles which keep it from fully evolving and accomplishing its spiritual mission. These obstacles appear as blockages and energetic crystallizations accumulated during this existence or others. These crystallizations can be of a spiritual, emotional, karmic, mental, or other, nature. They can also be the result of different types of trauma. The practices of intervention in spiritual angelic healing allow the different bodies to open, thus helping to free the soul's memories that are related to these crystallizations. A process of profound purification then begins, which helps the subject to become more and more open to the intervention process, and this helps the practitioner to dislodge the residue in the bodies of the person receiving the treatments.

Interventions are practiced on the median line of the subtle bodies. This line runs vertically, from the head to the feet of the physical body of a reclining subject and has a variable height according to the dimension of each of the subtle bodies.

Like a river holds water, this line holds the fluid of life, or prana. Prana circulates in the median line like water in a river bed. Just like water, the vital energy, or prana, encounters obstacles on its course: fissures, crevices, emotional rubble; densities, holes, gaps, karmic waterfalls; dams and obstructions; rigidities of the mind, divergences, weak currents, and spiritual dryness.

The training of practitioners in spiritual angelic healing makes them become a kind of geologist, archeologist, cave explorer, and even a geographer and historian of the soul and of the path which has been followed up until this moment. Its history is reconstructed with patience and with the help of the hands and body of the practitioner; by words perceived by the third ear; by visions and images of the third eye; by the emergence of scenes from this life and past lives; by information spontaneously transmitted by intuition, guides, and beings of light.

The subtle bodies of the subject naturally transmit these conscious or unconscious messages which, little by little, the practitioners learn how to receive as a result of their experience and their confidence in themselves as well as the process. These messages can be shared or not with the subject depending on his sensitivity, his openness to his own path, his evolution, and his self-knowledge. The power of the intervention is the result of three principle factors which, if they are very well synthesized, can create a perfect harmony. The first is the practitioner's capacity to become humble enough to be a simple channel of transmission and to refrain from getting caught up in the play of the mind and ego during the process; the second is simply the force of unconditional love and the energy of healing transmitted by the divine light which comes from the source; the third is the conscious collaboration of the subject because, as the angels tell us,

If a subject does not want to let go of his sadness, if he does not want to heal his anger, you cannot force him. If a subject does not want to participate in his healing and is not in a receptive state, you cannot induce healing. Thus for you < < saviors, > > you are going to lose your role, because you can't rescue the human race. Only the human himself can save himself.

The practitioner in spiritual angelic healing is a pure channel of light, love, and healing, accepting the call of his soul to offer a relief to human suffering.

There are different methods on earth of working with subtle bodies[2]. One method recommends acting on the core; another treats the periphery. The healing angels have observed that working on the median line is the quickest and most effective way because the information from the median line gives to the healer an immediate access to information about the global state of the being which would be difficult to see or impossible to obtain by the classical methods of investigation. It permits a wider vision of the interior reality of a person. Once the cause of disequilibrium is known, the healer, by his intervention, can stimulate or activate the inherent capacities of healing in the patient. This step gives the individual the ability to take a certain distance from his personal daily dramas and rediscover the goal of his existence.

---

[2]We must specify that during a treatment of spiritual angelic healing, the healer starts the intervention on the median line of the subtle body respecting the following order: etheric, emotional, mental, astral, supra-astral, celestial, body of light. The movement of the hands are done from top to bottom, in other words, from the crown chakra to the chakras below the feet.

Legend Of Configurations

Thin Line

Heavy Density

Mountains

Rubbles

Light Density

Gaps

Fissures and Crevices

Densities

A density is created when the prana which normally circulates freely in the median line experiences a contraction which hardens and solidifies it, to the point where it becomes compact and rooted in the depths of the median line, embedding itself in the core. Due to a wound like this, the being holds back energy as a protective reflex. The energy thus retained can no longer circulated freely, so it becomes hardened, creating a density. The densities found on the median line can vary in weight depending on the level of crystallization: from light to heavy.

Mountains, Holes, Mounds And Rubble

Considering the same type of wound, if the reaction to it is distorted, the energy accumulates on the exterior of the median line creating mountains, mounds, or rubble. If this expression of energy turns back on itself in a movement of self-destruction, this creates a hole.

A mountain is an accumulation of cells which have become hardened in a way different from that of a density. A mountain is less powerful than a strong density in terms of blocking energy.

Gaps

A gap is a hole, a lack. In the situation where there is a wound, the being collapses, retires, does not react; the movement of life is killed. This lack of nourishment creates a gap which resembles a chasm; the gap absorbs the prana, preventing the prana from nourishing the region of the median line affected by the reaction.

Fissures And Crevices

Fissures and crevices are leaks of energy created by doubts, incertitude, fear, hesitation, judgment, ambivalence and frustration. The prana is the vital energy, and each time you doubt, each time you are afraid, you weaken your vital energy. The weakening of the vital energy creates these crevices and fissures.

Weak Fluidity

When the fluidity is weak but the median line is normal, this weakness is not created by the presence of obstacles or configurations. It could be created by a shock, a sudden event, an important decision where the individual has no power. It could be created by a passive attitude toward life events and by a lack of taking charge. This passive retention progressively diminishes the circulating life energy, making the prana become sluggish as it circulates in the body. Weak fluidity can also be provoked by a state of pronounced fatigue leading to a depression of the nervous system and a lack of enough enthusiasm and energy to engage in action.

Thin Line With Fluidity

The impact of shock can create certain realities in the subtle bodies. It may be that the median lines and the bodies close themselves. After an accident or a shock it is possible to find very often a long line which has been tightened and which inhibits the pranic fluidity. It is very important to treat this line immediately, because if it is not treated, the core will not be nourished by the pranic fluid and will become crystallized.

Thin Line With Weak Fluidity

A median line which becomes very narrow and does not transport the vital fluid causes the body to become rigid and hardened, creating a kind of sarcophagus. At the extreme, the body becomes sunken onto the one underneath. This creates very serious illnesses which can even bring about a passing, or death.

Reversed Fluidity

Physical or emotional shocks of great importance can cause an inversion of the pranic fluidity: a plane crash, a very violent physical accident such as a train or car crash; an attack; the explosion of a bomb. If the subtle bodies are not treated after these incidents, it can lead to a reversal of the fluidity.

Certain factors of this reversal can equally come from the spiritual plane, such as the meeting of an earthly entity with a spiritual master through dreams or in reality. When a soul meets another soul more vibrationally evolved, it can create a reaction of the Kundalini and can even create a turmoil which reverses the pranic fluidity in the bodies affected by this meeting. Certain yogic practices done badly by the incarnated soul can also provoke a reversal of the pranic fluidity. Some physical exercises which violate gravitational power such as < <bungee jumping> > and < <free fall> > also interfere with the circulation of the pranic fluidity.

Parasites

Sometimes one may discover souls lying on a subject's subtle bodies or extending along the median lines of these bodies. These souls are vibrationally incompatible with the subject. They are present in order to take the energy of the subject, accompanying the subject during his or her earthly incarnation. These are known as parasites. The person carrying these souls accepted them on some level. There is neither a victim nor a persecutor. A person has parasites by his own consent, whether this consent is conscious or unconscious.

These souls which appear on the bodies are neither guides nor elevated souls or else they would not be acting as parasites. These souls are neither wicked nor bad: they are souls which wander in the earthly planes instead of going through the moment of passing, elevating themselves, and moving toward the light.

This obstacle called a parasite can never reach a subject's elevated bodies. One usually finds them no further than the astral body because the vibrational level of a subject's superior bodies does not permit the accumulation of parasites.

Parasites can only be thought-forms, which have encrusted themselves in the bodies. They are very restrictive and seem like a presence, which obstructs the prana and vital energy of the subject.

The closer the parasites are to the physical body, the more the subject who has them will feel a lack of drive, fatigue, and a loss of vital energy.

Chapter Six

The Relationship Between Configurations, Chakras, And Subtle Bodies

*W*e will now contemplate the different configurations and try to understand how they can occur. To facilitate the understanding, we will use the same example throughout. Let's take a chakra that probably speaks to most of us: the heart chakra.

First we have to grasp the interrelation that exists between each of the different bodies. We are not separated into closed compartments. We are a very well-interconnected energetic entity. What happens at one level of our being influences the whole. What happens in one subtle body influences the others.

With that in mind, we can begin with our example. We have a person with strong density over the heart chakra in the etheric body. We know that a density is a contradiction, a closing. We wouldn't be surprised if that person feels a tightening of his physical heart. If the density is present in the emotional body, that person will have the tendency to block his emotions related to the expression of love. In the mental body, a density indicates strong beliefs and/or conditioning regarding the free circulation and manifestation of love. A configuration in the astral body always indicates that the situation is related to and influenced by past life memories, and densities are no exception.

We continue the exploration with a mountain over the heart. First, this configuration tells us that there is an expression, an action: given a situation involving love, that person reacts. But that reaction is distorted, and so it creates a crystallization, a mountain. If it is found in the etheric body, we could have arrhythmia. In the emotional body, the healer may be able to read the emotions that were brought up by this situation, emotions such as anger, sadness, and so on. In the mental, we will be confronted by beliefs such as, < <One must beware of love, > > < <One must defend oneself against love. > > The memories of similar wounds can be found in the astral.

Now let's move on to the gaps. A gap is a hole, a lack, and it is a configuration that travels from one body to the next. If an individual has a gap on the heart chakra in the etheric body, you can be assured that there are deep wounds in the physical body. In the emotional, it tells you that the wounds are so strong that the person has totally cut himself off from love. In the mental, he has important believes concerning love such as, < <Love does not exist for me, > > < <Love is dangerous, > > and so on. In the astral, he has memories of having had his love energy wounded.

Let us stay with the example of the heart chakra and examine the three configurations we have up to now. Given a situation that triggers a wound related to love energy, we will have three different reactions. Someone with a density will close, harden his heart. The one with a mountain will react, defend the wound by an action or a word. The one with the gap will be crushed.

We now continue with the crevices and fissures. We have a person with fissures, and that tells us that we are in the presence

of someone with great fears, doubts, uncertainty or hesitations—
conscious or unconscious—concerning love. These attitudes will
be related to the physical, the emotional, the mental, or the astral
aspects of the person depending on which body they are located
in.

We will examine a last situation. We have someone with a
thin median line with weak fluidity. We have explained earlier
that the body with such a line can fall down onto the one
underneath. The consequences can vary in regard to which body
falls on which one.

If the etheric body becomes sunken onto the physical body,
you will feel a very great fatigue, black outs, and a total loss of
energy, leading to very serious illnesses and even death.

If it happens with the emotional body falling onto the etheric,
you will feel an important emotional disequilibrium which can
lead to psychosis or neurosis. The person can close himself off.

When the mental collapses on the emotional, it can create
symptoms described as mental illnesses. When the astral body
becomes sunken onto the mental body, this can cause a succession
of karmic falls. A karmic fall happens when the energy of a past
life becomes too heavy on the astral body. This causes this body
to fall and penetrate all of the other bodies, all the way down to
the physical one. Thus, that which was experienced in a past life
can recreate itself in this present existence.

Chapter Seven

Coma And Death

oma may be caused by the suffocation of the bodies due to a shock, or it can be caused by the destabilization of the bodies. After an accident or shock, the lines, if they are not healthy and have blockages, become fissured, distended, and open themselves. This can lead to death or clinical death, also known as coma. In order for a soul to leave the body, one must have all of his median lines separated and opened, so that the core can open itself and let the soul leave. Thus you cannot attempt to close the large lines of an entity who is dying. The entity is preparing himself to leave. This is why we angels repeat to humans that it is very important that the bodies are constantly energized during the incarnation on earth because the more the bodies are healthy, the easier it is for the entity to leave the planet Earth when it is time for him to leave. Souls have difficulty to leave when the subtle bodies are suffocated. For example, the soul tries to pass through the emotional, and the emotional restrains it because there is still too much anger and unresolved sentiments, so the soul cannot detach itself from all of the other bodies. Furthermore, if the astral body is too charged with unresolved feelings, the soul definitely can not ascend.

What happens when an entity leaves the earthly plane definitely? For the soul to leave, all of the bodies, all of the median lines must become separated. The cores must open themselves so that the soul can leave through the earthly body, then through the astral, and then join the celestial planes with his body of light which is his vehicle in the beyond. It is not the time to keep the lines together. To the contrary, you must place your hands of light and energize the separation so that the cores can breathe and the soul can leave in love. This is why the health of the subtle bodies is very important.

Imagine that a soul leaves and there are densities, gaps, and mountains, do you believe that soul can leave easily? That it will not be attached by a heavy sadness on the emotional body or a mountain formed by a system of beliefs which is crushing the plexus? In the moment of passing, that which holds the soul back is the attraction to staying on earth. The more the subtle bodies are healthy, the more the passing is easy.

The experience of an impact, an accident, or a shock can provide a scission in the subtle bodies if they are not in good health. The scission of the bodies can provoke the experience of coma where the soul goes to a certain place and experiences transmutation. There it can choose to come back into its physical form or not. During a coma we suggest, if it is at all possible and permitted by the medical institutions, to constantly check the state of the bodies, and if possible to help decrystallize them and to attempt to maintain the bodies and the pranic fluidity, no matter what the being has chosen, to live or not. When you are witness to a shock or death—if possibly—immediately put your hands on the bodies and energize them (project the light), to facilitate the passing of the return, because it's possible there will be a return, you never know! Either way, the placing of your hands will help.

If the soul must truly leave the earthly plane, it must be aided by guides and angels in order to fulfill all that has not been fulfilled in this incarnation during this first stage in the Passing.

Accompanying Those In The Process Of Dying

In my path, I have been called to help a couple of people during their last moments—people I had been treating during the preceding months. These experiences, because they were extremely touching moments for me, were great lessons of courage, surrender, detachment, and unconditional love. I was able to notice how necessary it is during our life to prepare for this last journey. Although death arouses a lot of apprehension, it is in fact only the passing of the soul to another plane. When a cycle of experiences has been completed, the soul chooses to leave its physical form. It is at this important moment that it must become detached and surrender everything that keeps it on the earth so that it can move toward the light.

One of the people I accompanied up until her last moments was named Suzanne. She had developed cancer. In spite of surgery and chemotherapy treatments, her state worsened and her illness, instead of going into remission, took over. Her fight to heal had lead her toward spirituality. During the year that had preceded her death, she had come to see me regularly. She had often expressed to me her fear of death and her desire to live. She had always suffered from a lack of love in her life, and she was sad at the thought that she was going to leave this life, never having known love.

Each time she received an intervention on her body she seemed more serene, more calm and could really experience love inside her. These interventions brought about a great opening of her consciousness, and she understood that she had chosen freely and that she had lived through certain experiences in order to liberate her soul from everything that was blocking its development. Even if my interventions were freeing her from buried memories, the illness continued to spread into all the cells of her body. During our last encounter, the spiritual guides of Suzanne gave me the message that her soul was soon going to leave her physical form. When I embraced all the bodies of light, I had the feeling of being surrounded by a shroud. A few months later, she called me from the hospital. She was living her last moments. She told me to come and sit by her side and accompany her up until the end. In passing my hands over her etheric body, I felt that her vital force was slowly leaving her physical body and her median line had become enlarged and had opened itself in order to allow her soul to leave.

Even if all the interventions that Suzanne had received had permitted her to free herself from a surplus of impressions and crystallizations which had weighed her down, during these last moments, her attachment to earthly life and to her loved ones kept her from being able to leave. In order to help her to achieve this ultimate passing, by continuing to transmit the light on her etheric body, I spoke with her soul and encouraged it to direct itself toward the light.

Suddenly, Suzanne became agitated all over and repeated, < <Close the zipper!> > She started to grab her covers and draw them to the center of her body as though to fill an invisible space. In fact, I saw that suddenly she wanted to close the median line which was becoming larger and larger in spite of her last resistances to leave her body. At this moment her children approached her and had one last exchange of affection with her, which was mixed with regret at not being able to share their love with her anymore. Then I saw the emotional body of Suzanne vibrating with a number of emotions, varying from attachment to sadness, from bitterness to disappointment, from regret to surrender. Then, calming herself, she joined her hands on her chest and said in a weak voice, < <I'm done.> > She asked me then to play the mantra *Om Namah Shivaya*, and peacefully she left.

I had been astonished and moved to see at that point that her face was beaming, freed from all the tensions and sufferings that she had experienced in her last moments. All her bodies, in fact, were bathed in a vibrant light. The room itself was filled with the sweet presence of the soul of Suzanne in the company of her guides. I said a last good-bye and encouraged her to ascend to the higher planes.

During the following days I felt a profound sadness at the thought that Suzanne had left us, but at the same time I was happy for her knowing that she was now free from her suffering.

I thanked her internally for having given me the permission to accompany her in her last journey, and I hoped I had done all that was possible to aid her soul to accomplish its passing. Absorbed in these thoughts I came home one night, and to my great surprise a magnificent bouquet of flowers was waiting for me on the table. Suzanne's children, whom I had met for the first time at the hospital, had sent me this gift for having taken care of their mother. For me it was as though she had offered these flowers in order to tell me that all had gone well.

One other time I was called to the bedside of a woman 30 years old. She also had attained cancer and was in the terminal phase. The doctors had not given her more than a few months to live. She welcomed me as her savior who had come to give her back her health, to save her from a certain death.

After having spoken with her for a long time, she confided to me that she had always been haunted by the fear of death. In the course of our encounters, I treated all of her subtle bodies, according to the angelic approach, and even though each treatment liberated her from a certain karmic baggage, I noticed that the cells of her body were dying, one after the other. On the astral plane her soul gave me the information that she must, during this present incarnation, completely liberate herself from the fear of death and to do this, paradoxically, by dying.

In explaining to her the path which must be accomplished by the soul in its voyage toward liberation, I brought to her all the spiritual help I could, right up until the end. The treatments permitted her to taste an interior peace and to open her consciousness to the possibility of a continuation of existence on other planes; this was something she had never considered before. This new conviction assured her a little bit. Up until her last moments she hoped to be able to heal her physical body, but little by little she resigned herself to the idea of leaving. At the moment when she accepted to make the transition, I saw two angels arrive who each took her by an arm and led her away.

Chapter Eight

Case Histories

*P*arallel to traditional doctors, there have always been healing shamans in our society. These doctors of the soul and of the body have developed the faculty to go to the other side of reality and to merge into the consciousness of another person. In this way, they have direct access to his spirit and his body and can perceive the invisible causes of his sickness or emotional disturbance.

In the course of my apprenticeship as healer I had been working on my own healing. Then I learned how to have access to the life plan of the people I was to accompany on the healing path.

This process was done in stages. It began by an exploration of my own subtle bodies during exercises of meditation. One day my breath spontaneously became more and more deep. At each inspiration and expiration I became more and more expanded. Then suddenly I became capable of perceiving my different bodies of energy. Gently, letting myself be transported by my breath, I raised myself through my different bodies one after the other. Each one appeared to be made of translucent bubbles, tainted by different luminous colors, and containing all sorts of emotions and vibrations corresponding to who I was as an individual.

Now when I treat another person I place myself vibrationally at the level of his energy and I project my consciousness on each one of his bodies. This permits me to perceive the median line, to question the body and to dialogue with it in order to find the source of disequilibrium from which he suffers. The goal of my interventions is to bring to the conscious level the unresolved problems which are blocking the fluidity of the energetic system and which can manifest themselves in the physical body by illnesses.

This has for an immediate effect a transformation, an opening of the consciousness of the subject, permitting him to see with a more evolved perspective, maybe for the first time in his life. Often spontaneously, by intuition, he sees which are the changes he must bring into his mode of life in order to bring about a larger well-being or better health. If he pursues this process, he can have better control of his life and can perceive that he is truly the master of his own destiny.

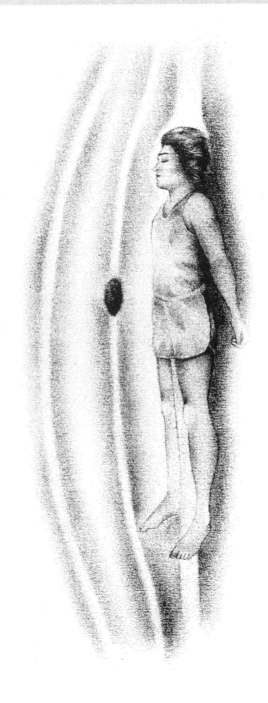

Exhaustion

Exhaustion

One day a man of about 40 years, in a state of advanced exhaustion, came to consult me. In order to soothe his discomfort, someone had prescribed tranquilizers, then he himself had tried certain mild medicines. The improvement had always been temporary. After an examination of the median line of his etheric body, which had become much too close to his physical body, I noticed that his energetic fluid was circulating very slowly and was becoming so dense that it called to mind the thickness of a stone, in the regions of the liver and the intestines.

This densification at the level of the physical body corresponded to the presence of intestinal parasites, difficult digestion, constipation, and a very bad elimination. I then, with the help of the angelic approach, proceeded to lift the etheric body in order to permit the cells of the core to be better nourished by the energy. And then I pushed aside and eliminated the density which had obstructed good circulation.

This intervention brought to this man a feeling of lightness and well-being, and a clarity of thought. He then realized the necessity of cleaning his digestive system, of purging his intestines, and of bettering his eating habits, notably in the consumption of fruit juice and fresh vegetables. In a short time he felt much better, and he had even decided to go further in his process toward better health.

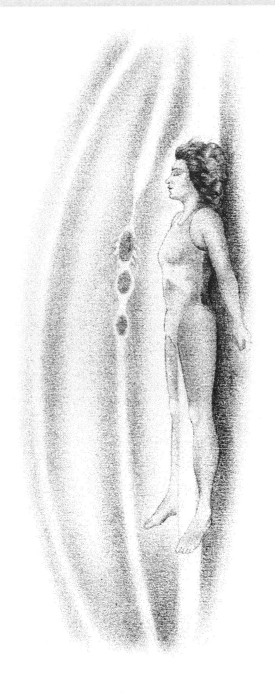

Hyperactive Thyroid

Hyperactive Thyroid

A young woman who thought that her thyroid gland was too active came to see me because she had been told to proceed with surgery in order to remove this gland. In passing my hands on the median line, I noticed that it was irregularly long in places, and that her energetic fluidity was very slow. I felt also that the chakras corresponding to the glands had been deeply blocked. On the throat chakra, I had the vision of an ancestor of this young woman who had suffered from goiter. This chakra was abnormally small, and the shrinkage of its base had invoked swelling at the level of its opening. The median line at this height was also very narrow. On her heart chakra appeared repressed emotions in her relationship with her mother. The rush of this mass of energy—which appeared to me to have a dark color—created fissures on the edges of the median line. The chakra of the solar plexus was impregnated with feelings of insecurity relating to fear of sickness. Many loved ones of this young woman suffered from cancer. Her digestion had been completely blocked which prevented her from having a good assimilation. Her etheric body was much too close to her physical body. This gave her the sensation of being crushed. At the chakra of the navel, I perceived that the young woman believed she should not manifest her femininity for fear of being wounded. This restraint caused a bad elimination which gave her a very stout figure. I realized then that this problem with the thyroid gland was a manifestation of a disequilibrium that I felt to be very serious. I suggested she should consult a doctor, who in turn diagnosed a cancer of the glandular system.

Sinusites and Multiple Allergies

Sinusitis And Multiple Allergies

A young man of 30 years suffering from sinusitis and multiple allergies came to see me. In passing my hands on his etheric body at the level of the head, I felt a barrage of dark thoughts related to a difficult relation with his father. The throat chakra which seemed to me abnormally small and closed was completely filled with mucus. In the region of the heart, the median line was riddled with obstacles resembling loose, large stones. These crystallizations corresponded to bitter, unresolved emotions relating to a previous existence where the young man had been an unhappy monk. At the level of his chakras, all of these emotions created a feeling of being strangled. This oppression blocked his respiration. The chakra of his solar plexus was dominated by feelings of anger mixed with fear of authority, sentiments which had been provoked by his dominating father. The liver, which is the organ most affected by anger, was in this case hardened and in a very bad state and could no longer fulfill its function as filter of the organism. The median line at this level appeared blocked by a black mass speckled with red: all of his emotions were repressed and affected his physical body and were, in my opinion, the cause of his allergies. In effect, when the mental body had become too thick, it sank onto itself and sank onto the emotional body bringing blockages which could manifest themselves as allergies.

Hysterectomy

Hysterectomy

A young woman who had been subjected to a hysterectomy showed on her median line at the height of the hara chakra a deep gap. On the affective plane, this gap corresponded to a feeling of guilt related to past lives where she had been a libertine. More or less consciously, in this life she held back her sensitivity and feminine sensuality. By filling this empty space with light and love, my intervention helped this person understand that she must love herself and forgive herself.

Multiple Schlerosis

Multiple Sclerosis

The etheric body of a man who had multiple sclerosis was only 10 centimeters (4 inches) away from the physical body. The median line had a good length: his guides had informed me that he had been a healer in other lives. The energetic fluidity, which usually circulates from the head to the feet, was reversed and weak. I felt that all of the cells were in an equal state. There had been a gap in the energetic flow at the level of the heart which corresponded to an emotional closing provoked by a very great, interior suffering. And there was another gap at the base chakra, representing an urge to die or an unconscious desire not to live. The core of the etheric body was speckled with small points of dark gray.

The median line of the emotional body seemed larger than that of the etheric body. However, the edges were red from anger and bitterness toward his father and toward God. The same gap at his heart and base chakras were present. The energetic fluid was very dense and a dark color. The core was tight and very rigid. My hands were pulled by the vacuum force of all these emotions.

The line of the mental body was very narrow and had fissures in places. The energetic current was practically dried up there. This corresponded in this man, on the psychological level, to a very great narrowness of spirit and a mental rigidity which had been his defense mechanism to avoid suffering. The mental activity took so much energy that there was only a little energy left at the base. From there the presence of this same gap was felt at the level of the first two bodies. The core of the mental body was heavy, like a block of cement, and pressed with all its weight onto the emotional body.

The astral body was charged with painful memories, very difficult to accept. I saw this man as a healer in his past lives sometimes abusing others with his power. I heard him even say in a strong and authoritarian voice, < <I am in control, and I won't let anyone walk all over me. > > In this life he had accepted to incarnate with great reticence. His soul knew that he had to progress, to accept not always being the first, to learn to surrender, to listen to others and to learn unconditional love. After a few visits, he felt the energy circulating in his legs which, until then, had been without feeling. He understood that he must continue to work on his healing, even if this process would turn out to be long, and he had to begin by accepting the fact that he really had wanted to go through this state and make himself better. As in most cases, this process of healing required that he re-contact and explore memories of his childhood and of certain past lives in order to liberate his behavior patterns and to transform them.

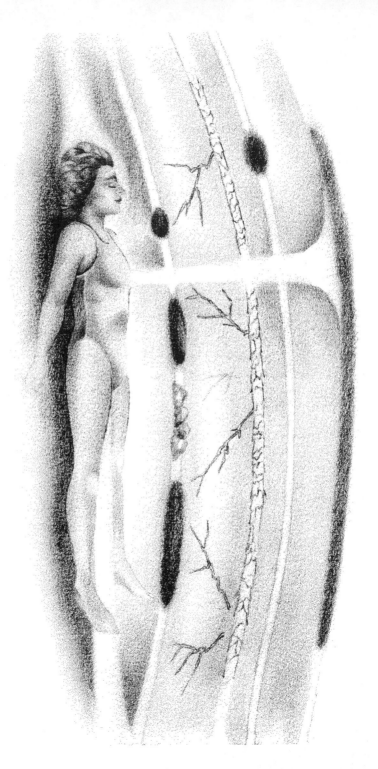

Bulimia

Bulimia

The median line of the etheric body of a woman suffering from bulimia was very narrow, and the energetic fluidity was very slow. Some densities appeared from the throat all the way to the feet. These configurations had the form of mountains which appeared between the thighs. The digestive system was irritated. Psychologically this woman, who had been subjected to incest from the most tender infancy, was experiencing enormous guilt, had a very low self-esteem, and a great fear of men.

The line of the emotional body was narrow, and the edges were fissured. There had been a great charge of electricity in the entire core of this body, a little bit like a sky heavily charged with energy and streaks of lightning before an electric storm. It was then that I understood the unconscious mechanism of her bulimia. When, during her childhood, her father abused her and then ordered her to say nothing to her mother under the pretext of not making her mother suffer, he forced her to repress her rage, her confusion, her fear, her shame, and her frustration. All of this energy had been accumulated at the unconscious level in her emotional body, but continued, nonetheless, to exist and to create a permanent emotional turbulence there. This constant emotional charge demanded an outlet—unexpected and sudden—in order to free itself. This is what had provoked the compulsive crisis of bulimia.

The median line of the mental body was also narrow with grayish densities around its head. This body was also very heavy and weighed on the emotional body. Her psyche was filled with guilt feelings and negative thoughts toward the world and her life.

It was at the level of the astral body that I made contact with her self-destructive behavior patterns. A density covered this body completely and hid a gap at the region of the astral heart and descended all the way to the physical heart. This gap corresponded to a lack of esteem, guilt, and a difficulty to accept this present incarnation which demanded that she work on her spiritual healing. After a few treatments, the bulimic crises diminished in their intensity and frequency. Feeling more integrated, she realized that she was more ready to take charge of herself without having to become dependent on others and to give them (even occasionally) all of her personal power. She was equally conscious that she had to forgive both herself and her father.

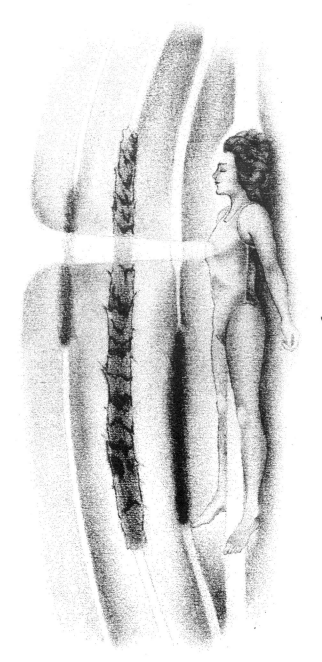

Sadness

Sadness

The median line of the etheric body of a 40-year-old woman suffering from a permanent feeling of sadness contracted itself from the heart to the plexus, and the edges were swollen in certain places. The tissue of the core around the head was grayish, and there was an energetic gap in the region of the heart. This corresponded to a great sadness caused by the fact that she always felt abandoned. From the navel all the way to her feet there had been a density reflected by a heavy and slow gait, denoting a languor and nonchalance. The chakra of the third eye was dark gray, flat and closed. This was the fear of recontacting certain sad memories relating to this problem of abandonment which had been the cause of this closure.

The emotional body showed a strong density on almost the entire length of the median line, whose edges were lightly fissured and were swollen. There, also, sadness was the dominant emotion and corresponded to the belief that her birth had not been wanted by her parents. The same gap was present at the level of her heart.

The median line of her mental body and her energetic fluidity was weak. A density was apparent from the throat to the base chakra where it inscribed itself as a feeling of resignation and submission. To avoid suffering, this person had become a prisoner in a restricted mental universe which limited her and blocked her from enlarging her experience of life.

The accumulated memories in the astral body which were crystallized weakened her energetic fluidity. At the level of her heart and plexus, I found the same gap. I felt that this soul had a great need to give and receive love. With my hands of light I took away the densities and gave to this median line a much bigger size. This person was suddenly encouraged and realized that her soul was continuing to work and get rid of these sentiments of rejection; she began to regain confidence in her personal capacities and to open herself to live fully. She then began to enlarge her field of activities, and today she is giving Reiki treatments to other people.

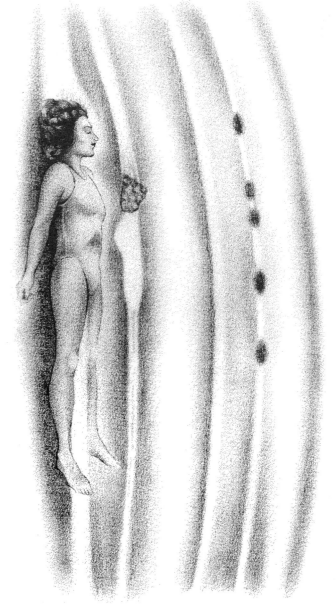

Anguish

Anguish

The median line of the etheric body of a woman suffering from anguish was narrow beginning at the knees and extending all the way to the feet. This person suffered from leg aches for no apparent reason. At the level of the heart, I felt a configuration similar to the form of a mountain representing repressed emotions which this woman did not want to express. This configuration was followed by a hole at the level of the solar plexus. This hole corresponded to the fear of being judged and criticized, which created a morbid fear of advancing in life.

The, emotional body was tainted with hot colors: red and yellow, representing all her anger and her repressed frustrations The energetic fluidity seemed as thick as black molasses, indicating a lack of joy of life, enthusiasm, liveliness, and lightness.

The mental body was filled with densities in the form of blocks representing defeatist beliefs and tendencies of self-destruction.

The astral body which had the consistency of cement was marked by the certitude that her life was a mistake. In effect, she was convinced that the guides from the beyond had made a mistake and that she had been pushed to incarnate on the earthly plane.

After many meetings, she understood that she had not been born by mistake, that she herself had chosen to come to the earth, and that she must assume responsibility for it and commit herself firmly to a direction in life. She is equally realizing that she must cease to think of projects automatically failing even before embarking upon them, and that it is in approaching life in a less dramatic fashion that she will be able to surmount her visceral fear of failure.

Endometriosis

Endometriosis

A young woman of 35 years, suffering from endometriosis, came to see me. She suffered from obesity, seemingly caused by retention of water and prolonged menstruations. After having proceeded with an examination of her etheric body, I noticed that her median line was coiled. This corresponded to a general disequilibrium responsible for a lot of fatigue and sluggishness. The energetic fluidity was slow and a lot of rubble obstructed her circulation at the level of the genital organs.

I suggested that this woman was unconsciously repressing her feminine energy because her mother, during her pregnancy, had wanted a boy. It's important to note also that this young woman of Asian origin had, during her youth, endured a prolonged detention in a concentration camp. Her emotional body, by consequence, had been marked by extreme feelings of regret and sadness which enveloped her like a dark layer. What's more, it was full of parasites caused by the suffering of the other people who had lived in the same camp. I felt that I could even hear moaning, cries, and lamentations. Not having been able to help the other prisoners had filled her with guilt and powerlessness.

The median line of the mental body was narrow, and the sides were hard. This rigidity came from the belief that life is difficult and necessarily filled with suffering and that it is a heavy weight to carry.

On the astral body I felt the presence of all her people, whose condition permanently haunted her. This woman was literally oppressed by the unconscious collective of her nation. I perceived her in her past lives as socially very important, very authoritative, and utilizing her power to abuse and dominate. Her soul informed me that in this present incarnation she had chosen to play the role of the victim in order to equalize her karma. What's more, she had to learn to forgive her mother who had abandoned her during her childhood and sent her to live in a foreign country.

During these treatments, I freed her somewhat from the unconscious collective of her people which were becoming like parasites on her bodies. I also suggested to her that she follow a regime of physical exercise. The loss of blood and the swelling diminished. Understanding that she must make peace with her past and let go, she learned how to face her life with much more serenity.

Chapter Nine

Personal Shares

The personal shares which follow come from people who have given or received treatments of spiritual angelic healing.

< <Each time that I intervene with spiritual angelic healing, I am in contact with a subtle universe of energy. I enter into the vast history of this being before me, and seeing how the love that I channel through my hands is unconditional, I don't know in which manner the energy is going to act nor how it will be received.

For the last four years I have witnessed physical and emotional healing. It seems that in all the cases I have been a witness to the process of spiritual healing. In his words and attitude, the person always expresses a great opening, a larger receptivity, and a greater recognition of his divine nature.

A recent concrete example is that of a man of 40 years, extremely agitated and anxious. Since the age of 16, he took < <medication> > for his nerves, as he called it. Following our first intervention of spiritual angelic healing on the seven subtle bodies, he said that he felt a great improvement. His spouse gave me many examples which demonstrated how he had changed. His spouse repeated that she found him unrecognizable, and that he had diminished his medications. These experiences always make me feel profoundly grateful. > >

—*Yvette, psychologist*

< < The treatments of spiritual angelic healing have permitted me to live a renaissance. Now I have the impression of living fully in my physical body, and I perceive it like a vehicle. I have found a joy of living, interior peace, and sometimes I even have moments of ecstasy. I feel more detached in the face of events in this existence. I live fully in the present moment, and I surrender myself more and more to that which the universe brings to me. > >

—*Nicole, professional*

< < The interventions of spiritual angelic healing exist in order to carry out the intention of bringing celestial energies onto the earthly plane. There are different gestures, just as there are different intentions. One must always fill one's gestures with the energy of love in order to succeed in letting the healing happen.

These treatments of spiritual angelic healing provoke an awakening in the person who receives them, an awakening of the belief in the existence of energy. From there, one begins to sharpen one's questioning and pose serious questions about what one does on this earth.

The first treatment I received gave me a great revelation. It was as though I had been split in two. This feeling helped me to establish my belief in spiritual angelic healing and its effectiveness. I could not believe it. No one touched me, and it was still so powerful.

Spiritual angelic healing was an experience. If it had not been my own experience, I would have never been touched by it. Listening to people speak about it was not sufficient. I had to live it. After having experienced it, it was totally another story. It was magic. It gave me the desire to become a magician.

I discovered at the same time my capacity to feel energy. When I met the angels for the first time, it was in 1994 at a public meeting. I tasted the energy. I received a shower of energy. I was assisting at the conference, just to listen. I hadn't yet heard anything, and I received a vibrational shock. This has truly stayed with me, this feeling of energy which hit me. I was so skeptical, so stuck in the mind. The angels used the method perfectly suited to touch me. I had a resistance to it. I was part of the business world. It was necessary for me to have a strong experience. Otherwise I would have given up.

Now, I am able to perceive things before they happen. I am able to feel my emotions more now. Being guided on this path has helped me understand how to put words to what I'm feeling. I've always had confidence in what I do; I'm trying to say that now I am an addict of divine energy. I'm trying to say that the energy of the angels comes from the Source. There is only one energy, the energy of love.

I notice when I am in a space of love that the energy takes on another color. When I am not in a space of inner love when making the healing gestures and rituals, the divine energy does not go as well. I don't feel as well.

I know that it's pompous to say, but there is an extraordinary side to this. One must experience it in order to be able to understand it. Putting words on an experience like this already lessens the reality. In spiritual angelic healing, I enter into a world where words are superfluous when trying to qualify what I do. Spiritual angelic healing is an apprenticeship. I feel that more and more. I also feel that the channeling has become more and more powerful. I do interventions today that I was totally incapable of doing four months ago. I have the impression of becoming more precise, more efficient with practice. There are never two people who have the same reaction. > >

—*Saul, businessman*

< < The first time that I received a treatment of spiritual angelic healing was in a training course where I had accepted to be a subject. I was overwhelmed when I heard the two practitioners identify and name the most profound wounds of my life when they didn't even know me. I asked them how they had been able to make such profound contact with my intimate personal history, simply by passing their hands above my body. I was even more moved when they began to treat my wounds.

I felt an opening, a profound liberation, the impression of being able to breathe better, throughout all my being. As I cried, I felt an incredible peace installing itself little by little in all my cells. This peace was accompanied by an intense vibration of love. At this moment, the Angels Xedah, through the medium of Marie Lise Labonté, came near me, saying, < < You are more at peace than you would ever believe. > >

The peace was quickly followed by an irresistible joy which made me smile, then burst out in laughter like a child. I had the crazy wish to go, in my clothes, and plunge in the pool under the radiant sun of the Dominican Republic where the training was taking place. The embrace, the sweetness, and the heat of the water completed this first treatment which I will always remember.

—*Sarah, psychotherapist*

< < The interventions of spiritual angelic healing raise our consciousness and permit a free circulation of love and light in our entire body. They open us to a new dimension and put us into contact with this immensity of love which lives inside us. They bring us to our own divine essence, our own truth. This is what guides my life now.

To transmit these interventions creates in me an expansion and gives me a great desire to love totally. That which I offer to my clients is the sharing of this dimension in all its simplicity and all its humility, in a place of no expectations, in the unconditional, with respect for these sacred rituals.

I wish that each of you can savor this transmission of energy and, in your turn, profit from this immeasurable experience of communion with the Source.

—*Suzanne, Reiki master*

< < In choosing to be trained in spiritual angelic healing, I touched my soul, and I had the experience of the invisible and of God . . . God in me, outside of all systems of beliefs and all desires to impose my experiences on another.

I understood that the healer acts by love which emanates from him, and with this love he accomplishes both great and small feats. The inner space where I am when I practice spiritual angelic healing vibrates with an omnipresent thought of love which makes me see my own delusion when I cease to be filled with love. And I simultaneously receive and transmit this love which heals without conditions. It's incredible. > >

—*Sylvie, Doctor*

< < I felt spiritual angelic healing like a call, a call of the soul, without any logical or reasonable reference, save that my hands always wanted to do something like this!

What a beautiful, strange, and fascinating adventure where everything, absolutely everything, invited me to change the way I saw the world, these beings, and even my own self! The joy of surrender!

Spiritual angelic healing permitted me to re-contact the dimension for which I had long been searching and to get to know myself again at the same time. Oh, what great luck! This tool of healing, incredibly beautiful and magnificently simple, is equally equipped with an infinite intelligence: the subtle bodies know and inform us constantly. To be tuned into the bodies and to act on them in order to help them become liberated, light, more balanced, and thus to relocate their light and their connection with the Source is, for some of us, to risk becoming completely intoxicated!

These subtle bodies which nourish and protect our physical form tell our history, all of its nooks and crannies, in a language which is very simple. Each meeting is, however, a meeting of the unknown, in total surrender. These moments of sharing with the essential are a royal path to the unconditional and love.

My experience with spiritual angelic healing turned out to be a point of departure a true personal revolution. Even though I had a sincere and profound desire to help people find in themselves and through themselves their light and their own path of healing, to have total confidence in my hands and my intuition was still a considerable job for me, and one which I had not yet truly acquired.

To begin with, I was afraid of making mistakes, of letting people down, of not being efficient, of not being loving or giving. The feeling of losing my personal identity was difficult to deal with; the confrontation with my own inner judge and all these exterior mirrors of skepticism, astonishment and doubt, reflected my own difficulty to recognize myself as an instrument of love and light. But this path my soul is on always succeeded in helping me break through. > >

—*Mukta, teacher*

Epilogue

ealing is unconditional because you know, in the deepest part of your heart, that there is one sole and unique vibration which permits the circulation of healing energy. This vibration is called love. Once again, we speak to you about love. Maybe we're repeating endlessly, but we are going to continue until all humans know experientially, and not just intellectually, the vibration of love. You have the capacity to channel unconditional love through your sushumna, because your soul is inhabited by a divine essence. You have this divine essence in you, and thus it is possible, in each second, to experience that there is no separation between you and the divine source. It is only through love that it is possible to experience the unconditional.

Recognize that you are love. You are the incarnated soul who is having an apprenticeship on earth. And this apprenticeship is not separate from the divine source. This apprenticeship is done through the experience of the divine source. You are much more vast than your physical form which serves you as a vehicle for growth. This is why it is very important to love your physical form and help it to heal itself. Healing is a vibrational state without conditions.

Certain humans believe that tools can heal. Tools are not channels. If you give tools the power of healing in place of giving yourself this power, the tools can not heal you. Only the soul knows, in all its divine power, where its healing dwells. Love the spaces in you which you call weak. Love the parts of your physical body that you judge weak. Love the cells of your body which you call < <destroyers. > > Love the parts of your physical body which suffer. Love the spaces of non-love in you. Non-love leads to destruction, and love leads to re-construction.

The entity who suffers needs love. The entity who suffers searches to nourish himself with energy. You can choose to transmit love. However, we are asking that your love be without conditions. If you merge with beings who are suffering, the unconditional is necessary. Don't judge suffering. Give love to suffering. Suffering is created by cellular vibrational spaces in your body, in the experience of your soul where there has been a non-love.

Love diminishes suffering because it sends a vibration into the cells which have experienced non-love, however, you can also give this love to yourself. That is healing.

When someone gives unconditional love to those who are suffering, that, too, is healing. In this experience of the unconditional, the one who chooses to transmit the unconditional acts also on himself. This is how unconditional healing creates a chain of energy. This is how unconditional healing can, by human action, spread its vibrational energy throughout the planet.

Conclusion

In the magical and mysterious universe of spirituality, it is said that beings of light are here to offer their inspiration and their protection to humanity. These beings bring support and comfort to all the souls who search for light on the earth. These beings of light called angels of healing have come here at the end of this century to transmit a teaching to us that will permit us to enlarge our consciousness, giving us a larger vision so that we will know healing. They send a powerful ray of light into us which can penetrate the inner sanctuary of our hearts.

We are presently living in a phase of evolution which leads us to contemplate all the aspects of our existence. Everything that blocks the process of transformation must be swept out of our lives. It is now time to act from our hearts and not from our minds which are often based on a system of beliefs of fear and non-love. In order to do it, we must first of all heal all the wounds of our hearts which have been accumulating for a long time. We must also let go of the attachment to these wounds in order to allow our hearts to breathe with love, because attachment creates suffering.

Sadness and suffering are common lines which unite all human beings. We all carry, deeply in our hearts, a great wound. This wound is the sadness of the separation from our true identity. This separation cuts us off from the source of love that is within us. During our voyage on earth, we are constantly searching for this love outside of us. Now it is time to heal the spaces of our hearts which have been wounded.

Spiritual angelic healing is there to help us in our process of healing. It activates the natural skill of the heart to heal itself and to nourish the parts of our being which have felt abandoned. Spiritual angelic healing helps us let go of these wounds and learn to love in a new way. It gives us access to a higher level of consciousness and helps us experience the transmutation of the Soul and the opening of the heart. It is a ray of hope which brings us a vision beyond our limitations. If we can accept the divine aspect of our being, our lives will be more harmonious and with time we will realize that we are not human beings who have spiritual experiences, but spiritual beings who have human experiences.

In this end of the century, spiritual angelic healing offers us the opportunity to explore the secret facets of our soul and to complete an important cycle of growth. When we emerge from our old wounds, we will have a new outlook on life, like a butterfly who miraculously leaves his cocoon.

From the bottom of my heart, I thank all of the souls who have chosen me as a guide in their path toward healing and transformation. Each one of these encounters allows me to grow through this process and to experience yet again a surrendering to grace.

I hope that all of the information contained in this work will be an inspiration for you on the path of healing.

Glossary Of Terms

Antigymnastics: Psychotherapeutic approach of the body created by movements works called < <prealables> > that releases the deep tensions and the emotional memories located in the cells of the body's muscles. This approach is a holistic one which see the body having a mind by itself and the mind having a body. This work has been created in Europe 20 years ago.

Chakra: Centers of energy within the body.

Channel: To direct the energy of those in a higher plane through a person on the earthly plane (a medium).

Kundalini: Subtle form of primordial energy which lies like a sleeping snake at the root of the spine. When this energy is awakened by spiritual practices, it can be experienced as a sacred fire climbing along the spine through the central channel (sushumna) and cleansing every thing on its way.

Endometriosis: The presence of uterine lining in other pelvic organs, especially the ovaries, characterized by cyst formation, adhesions, and menstral pains.

Hara: Japanese name given to the second chakra (the navel area) center of inner power and creativity.

Karuna: Spiritual name given by a spiritual master meaning the universal compassion of the Bodhisattva.

Medium: Someone who acts as a mouthpiece for entities who cannot appear in the human form.

Prana: Universal life force present in the air.

Reiki: Healing energy transmitted through an initiation, after which the practionner transferred the healing energy by putting his hands on the body.

Sushumna: The circuit of energy situated along the spinal column allowing the awakening of the Kundalini energy.

Yogic: School of Hindu philosophy advocating and prescribing a course of physical and mental disciplines for attaining liberation from the material world and a union of the self with the Supreme Being or ultimate principle.

Marie Lise Labonté

Author, psychotherapist, channel & co-founder of The Anschma International School for Energetic Health.

Marie Lise Labonté, M.O.A., a speech and hearing therapist and a psychotherapist, became interested in the body-mind connection as a result of a serious illness which stuck her in 1974. In 1980, she created a method of healing called < <The Global Approach to the Body> > which combines a psycho-corporal approach with the visualizing techniques of Doctor Carl Simonton. After years of research and spending time with people who were diagnosed with illnesses such as cancer, arthritis, multiple sclerosis and Aids, Marie Lise began to realize the importance of spiritual development in the healing process. It was at this moment she received the grace of the Healing Angels Xedah and spontaneously began channeling. At their demand, she co-found the Anschma International School for Energetic Health which offers training, throughout Canada, Europe and the United States in the disciplines set forth by the Healing Angels.

Marie Lise Labonté is the author of several books written by her and the channel of many other books relating to the Angelic Wisdom.

Books Marie Lise has written:

S'Autoguerir, c'est possible! (Heal Yourself; It's Possible!) Québec/Amérique Publications, 1986

L'Antigymnastique, une nouvelle approche du corps (Antigymnastics, A New Approach to the Body) Québec/Amérique Publications, 1991

Ces Vois qui me parlent (These Voices Who Speak To Me) Shanti Publications, 1993

La danse du funambule sur la Voie de l'Amour (The Dance of the Tightrope Walker on the Path of love) Shanti Publications, 1996

Marie Lise is the channel for this book:

Conversations With Angels Blue Pearl Press, 1998

Ninon Prévost

Master teacher. Author. Healer.

Ninon Prévost has worked in the field of healing and personal development for many years. Her work lead her to explore basic disciplines which improve the individual's physical, mental, and spiritual well-being. She made many long visits to the United States and India, spending time in the company of true masters of yoga and meditation.

Ninon has studied hypnotherapy, naturopathy, and Reiki. She is a member of the Canadian Professional Order of Naturopaths. She has been trained to do Reiki and became a Reiki Master within the Reiki Association Alliance. She has a certificate from the Academy of Advanced Healing Art of New Mexico and is a fitness and nutrition consultant. Ninon has been interviewed a number of times on television and radio, and she has written articles on the subject of healing for specialized journals.

After being initiated into the teachings of the Angels Xedah, Ninon became a master teacher in spiritual healing and past life regression.

Ninon teaches the discipline of spiritual healing, which is known as energetic therapy in Canada and the Caribbean. She also organizes pilgrimages to different parts of the world which have a particularly high sacred energy.

Ninon founded the Mariposa Foundation in Montréal, a non-profit organization which makes treatments in energetic therapy available to those who do not have sufficient financial resources.

Ninon is recognized for her professional competence, her earnestness, her devotion, and her commitment to soothing those who suffer. In this book, one finds the culmination of her experiences with the many people who inspired her to share this information, and one benefits from her own personal search as well.

For Those Who Feel The Call To Heal

Courses in Energetic Therapy

During week long sessions, you will discover how to channel the divine angelic healing energy. Using your own type of perception you learn how to touch, feel, and heal the subtle bodies. Students do hands-on, practical exercises and spend hours of meditation, prayer, contemplation, and discussion together.

Courses in Past Life Regression

To fully understand and direct the healing process, it is important to learn the affects of past lives on the present one. In this course, we learn how to guide a person through the healing of past life wounds and bring their awareness to the karmic lessons available in this very lifetime. By facing courageously these karmic lessons, the individual can actually facilitate the soul's evolution.

Marie Lise Labonté & Ninon Prévost can offer training sessions in energetic therapy and past life regression anywhere in the world.

For more information about these courses please call:

Anschma School for Energetic Health

1-514-841-9952
www.anschma.com

Ninon Prévost
1-888-369-1515
C.P. 112
Lasalle,
Quebec, H8R 3T3
Canada

BOOKS THAT CAN TRANSFORM LIVES

Conversations With Angels
Marie Lise Labonte
This best-selling book is comprised of transcriptions
of teachings given by the Angels Xedah that teach
us about love, forgiveness and more.

Big Medi$in
Bertram Wong
A humorous, honest and sometimes painful expose
of mainstream medicine. The author offers unique
and powerful insights designed to save your life.

Chronicles of Light
Earl Simmons, M.D.
Extraordinary testimonials of a doctor who
actually heals through the laying-on of hands.

God In A Black Jag
Timothy Ernster
A compelling story of one man's tranformational
journey taking him from a life focused on
success in the business world to a life
focused on self-realization.

Heart to Heart
Gilles Deschênes
Dialogues and exercises that develop the capacity
for truly experiencing unconditional love.

NOW AVAILABLE THROUGH

1-888-BOOKS-08